D0231833

Poet to Poet
George Herbert Selected by W. H. Auden

GEORGE HERBERT (1593–1633) studied at Trinity
College, Cambridge, where he was appointed Reader of
Rhetoric (1618) and Public Orator (1620). He was elected
to Parliament in 1624, but two years later resigned from
civil employment and took orders. He died in 1633 of
consumption. His book, *The Temple*, which includes
practically all of his surviving English poems, was first
published before the end of that year.

WYSTAN HUGH AUDEN was born in York in 1907 and
went up to Oxford in 1925. In 1939 he settled in the
United States. His first major collection, *Poems*, was
published in 1930. During that period he was closely
associated with Christopher Isherwood, Stephen Spender,
Louis MacNeice and Cecil Day Lewis. He has since
published numerous collections of poetry and critical
essays and has edited a great number of anthologies of
poetry and prose. He has also written (in collaboration
with Chester Kallman) opera librettos, the most famous
of which is for Stravinsky's opera *The Rake's Progress*. He
is the most prolific and accomplished poet writing in
English in the twentieth century.

GEORGE HERBERT

Selected by
W. H. Auden

Penguin Books

Penguin Books Ltd, Harmondsworth,
Middlesex, England
Penguin Books Inc., 7110 Ambassador Road,
Baltimore, Maryland 21207, U.S.A.
Penguin Books Australia Ltd, Ringwood,
Victoria, Australia

First published 1973
Selection copyright © Penguin Books Ltd, 1973
Copyright © 1973 in all countries of the International
Copyright Union by W. H. Auden

Made and printed in Great Britain by
Cox & Wyman Ltd, London, Reading and Fakenham
Set in Monotype Ehrhardt

Contents

Contents

Introduction

Reading a poet whose work I admire, it is only very seldom that I find myself wishing: 'Oh, how I would like to have been an intimate friend of his!' There are some, like Byron, whom I would like to have met once, but most, I feel, would either, like Dante and Goethe, have been too intimidating, or, like Wordsworth, too disagreeable. The two English poets, neither of them, perhaps, major poets, whom I would most like to have known well are William Barnes and George Herbert.

Even if Isaak Walton had never written his life, I think that any reader of his poetry will conclude that George Herbert must have been an exceptionally good man, and exceptionally nice as well.

He was born in Montgomery Castle on 3 April 1593, the fifth son of Sir Richard Herbert and Lady Magdalen Herbert, to whom Donne dedicated his elegy 'Autumnal Beauty', and his uncle was Lord Herbert of Cherbury. By birth, that is to say, he enjoyed a secure social position. In addition Nature had endowed him with the gifts of intelligence and personal charm. Educated at Westminster School and Trinity College, Cambridge, he became a Fellow of the latter in 1616, and was appointed Public Orator to the University in 1620. He was not only an excellent Greek and Latin scholar, but also fluent in Italian, Spanish and French, and an accomplished amateur musician who played the lute and composed songs.

For a young man of his breeding and talents one would have prophesied a great future in the world. He soon attracted the attention of two powerful and influential figures, the Duke of

Richmond and the Marquess of Hamilton and, when they met, King James I took great fancy to him.

His own ambition was as great as his opportunities. He seems to have dreamed of one day becoming a Secretary of State and this led him somewhat to neglect his duties as Public Orator in order to attend the Court. The Academic Life, evidently, was not altogether to his taste. Walton tells us:

... he had often designed to leave the university, and decline all study, which he thought did impair his health; for he had a body apt to a consumption, and to fevers, and other infirmities, which he judged were increased by his studies ... But his mother would by no means allow him to leave the university or to travel; and though he inclined very much to both, yet he would by no means satisfy his own desires at so dear a rate as to prove an undutiful son to so affectionate a mother.

This is confirmed in the poem 'Affliction'.

> Whereas my birth and spirit rather took
> > The way that takes the town;
> Thou didst betray me to a lingring book,
> > And wrap me in a gown.
> I was entangled in the world of strife,
> Before I had the power to change my li .
>
> Yet, for I threatned oft the siege to raise,
> > Not simpring all mine age,
> Thou often didst with Academick praise
> > Melt and dissolve my rage.
> I took thy sweetned pill, till I came where
> I could not go away, nor persevere.

Though he writes in another poem, 'The Pearl':

> I know the wayes of Pleasure, the sweet strains,
> The lullings and the relishes of it;
> The propositions of hot bloud and brains;

one does not get the impression from his work that the

temptations of the flesh were a serious spiritual menace to him, as they were to Donne. Nor did he suffer from religious doubts: in the seventeenth century very few people did. His struggle was with worldliness, the desire to move in high circles, to enjoy fame and power, and to such temptations he might very well have succumbed, had not his two aristocratic patrons and then, in 1625, King James, all died, thus dashing his hopes of immediate preferment.

For the first time he began to consider seriously the possibility of taking Holy Orders, a course which his mother had always prayed for. Most of his friends disagreed, thinking the priesthood too mean an employment, too much below his birth and natural abilities. To one such counsellor, he replied:

It hath been formerly adjudged that the domestic servants of the King of heaven should be of the noblest families on earth; and though the iniquity of the late times have made clergymen meanly valued, and the sacred name of priest contemptible, yet I will labour to make it honorable by consecrating all my learning, and all my poor abilities, to advance the glory of that God that gave them.

These words show that Herbert was under no illusion as to the sacrifice he would have to make, and to come to a definite decision was clearly a struggle, for he was not ordained a priest until 1630 when he was made Rector of Bemerton, a tiny rural parish on Salisbury Plain. In the previous year he had married Jane Danvers after a courtship of only three days, and the marriage turned out to be a very happy one. In 1633 he died of consumption at the age of only forty.

Since none of his poems were published during his lifetime, we cannot say for certain when any of them were written, but one suspects that it was from the two and a half years of indecision that many of them, particularly those which deal with temptations and feelings of rebellion, must date.

Since all of Herbert's poems are concerned with the religious life, they cannot be judged by aesthetic standards alone. His

poetry is the counterpart of Jeremy Taylor's prose: together
they are the finest expressions we have of Anglican piety at its
best. Donne, though an Anglican, is, both in his poems and his
sermons, much too much of a *prima donna* to be typical.

Comparing the Anglican Church with the Roman Catholic
Church on the one hand and the Calvinist on the other,
Herbert writes:

> A fine aspect in fit aray,
> Neither too mean, nor yet too gay,
> > Shows who is best.
> Outlandish looks may not compare:
> For all they either painted are,
> > Or else undrest.
>
> She on the hills, which wantonly
> Allureth all in hope to be
> > By her preferr'd,
> Hath kiss'd so long her painted shrines,
> That ev'n her face by kissing shines,
> > For her reward.
>
> She in the valley is so shie
> Of dressing, that her hair doth lie
> > About her eares:
> While she avoids her neighbours pride,
> She wholly goes on th' other side,
> > And nothing wears.

Herbert, it will be noticed, says nothing about differences in
theological dogma. The Anglican Church has always avoided
strict dogmatic definitions. The Thirty-Nine Articles, for
example, can be interpreted either in a Calvinist or a non-
Calvinist sense, and her Office of Holy Communion can be
accepted both by Zwinglians who regard it as a service of
Commemoration only, and by those who believe in the Real
Presence. Herbert is concerned with liturgical manners and
styles of piety. In his day, Catholic piety was typically baroque,

both in architecture and in poets like Crashaw. This was too unrestrained for his taste. On the other hand, he found the style of worship practised by the Reformed Churches too severe, too 'inward'. He would have agreed with Launcelot Andrewes who said: 'If we worship God with our hearts only and not also with our hats, something is lacking.' The Reformers, for instance, disapproved of all religious images, but Herbert thought that, on occasions, a stained-glass window could be of more spiritual help than a sermon.

> Doctrine and life, colours and light, in one
> When they combine and mingle, bring
> A strong regard and aw; but speech alone
> Doth vanish like a flaring thing,
> And in the eare, not conscience ring.

Walton tells us that he took enormous pains to explain to his parishioners, most of whom were probably illiterate, the significance of every ritual act in the liturgy, and to instruct them in the meaning of the Church Calendar. He was not a mystic like Vaughan: few Anglicans have been. One might almost say that Anglican piety at its best, as represented by Herbert, is the piety of a gentleman, which means, of course, that at its second best it becomes merely genteel.

As a Christian, he realized that his own style of poetry had its spiritual dangers:

> . . . Is there in truth no beautie?
> Is all good structure in a winding stair?

But as a poet he knew that he must be true to his sensibility, that all he could do was to wash his sweet phrases and lovely metaphors with his tears and bring them

> to church well drest and clad:
> My God must have my best, even all I had.

He is capable of writing lines of a Dante-esque directness. For example:

> Man stole the fruit, but I must climb the tree,
> The Tree of Life to all but only Me.

But as a rule he is more ingenious, though never, I think, obscure.

> Each thing is fully of dutie:
> Waters united are our navigation;
> Distinguished, our habitation;
> Below, our drink; above, our meat;
> Both are our cleanlinesse. Hath one such beautie?
> Then how are all things neat?

He is capable of clever antitheses which remind one of Pope, as when, speaking of a woman's love of pearls for which some diver has risked his life, he says:

> Who with excessive pride
> Her own destruction and his danger wears.

And in a most remarkable sonnet, 'Prayer', he seems to foreshadow Mallarmé.

> Church-bels beyond the starres heard, the souls bloud,
> The land of spices; something understood.

Wit he had in abundance. Take, for example, 'The Church-Porch'. Its subject matter is a series of moral maxims about social behaviour. One expects to be utterly bored but, thanks to Herbert's wit, one is entertained. Thus, he takes the common-place maxim, 'Don't monopolize the conversation', and turns it into:

> If thou be Master-gunner, spend not all
> That thou canst speak, at once; but husband it,
> And give men turns of speech: do not forestall
> By lavishnesse thine own, and others wit,
>   As if thou mad'st thy will. A civil guest
>   Will no more talk all, then eat all the feast.

A good example of his technical skill is the poem 'Denial'. He was, as we know, a skilled musician, and I am sure he got the idea for the structure of this poem from his musical experience of discords and resolving them. The first five stanzas consist of a quatrain, rhymed *abab*, followed by a line which comes as a shock because it does not rhyme:

> O that thou shouldst give dust a tongue
> > To crie to thee,
> And then not heare it crying! all day long
> > My heart was in my knee,
> > > But no hearing.

But in the final stanza the discord is resolved with a rhyme.

> O cheer and tune my heartlesse breast,
> > Deferre no time;
> That so thy favours granting my request,
> > They and my minde may chime,
> > > And mend my ryme.

This poem and many others also show Herbert's gift for securing musical effects by varying the length of the lines in a stanza. Of all the so-called 'metaphysical' poets he has the subtlest ear. As George Macdonald said of him:

The music of a poem is its meaning in sound as distinguished from word ... The sound of a verse is the harbinger of the truth containedin it ... Herein Herbert excels. It will be found impossible to separate the music of his words from the music of the thought which takes shape in their sound.

And this was Coleridge's estimate:

George Herbert is a true poet, but a poet *sui generis*, the merits of whose poems will never be felt without a sympathy with the mind and character of the man.

My own sympathy is unbounded.

W. H. AUDEN

The Church-Porch

1

Thou, whose sweet youth and early hopes inhance
Thy rate and price, and mark thee for a treasure;
Hearken unto a Verser, who may chance
Ryme thee to good, and make a bait of pleasure.
    A verse may finde him, who a sermon flies,
    And turn delight into a sacrifice.

2

Beware of lust: it doth pollute and foul
Whom God in Baptisme washt with his own blood.
It blots thy lesson written in thy soul;
The holy lines cannot be understood.
    How dare those eyes upon a Bible look,
    Much lesse towards God, whose lust is all their book?

3

Abstain wholly, or wed. Thy bounteous Lord
Allows thee choise of paths: take no by-wayes;
But gladly welcome what he doth afford;
Not grudging, that thy lust hath bounds and staies.
    Continence hath his joy: weigh both; and so
    If rottennesse have more, let Heaven go.

4

If God had laid all common, certainly
Man would have been th' incloser: but since now
God hath impal'd us, on the contrarie
Man breaks the fence, and every ground will plough.
  O what were man, might he himself misplace!
  Sure to be crosse he would shift feet and face.

5

Drink not the third glasse, which thou canst not tame,
When once it is within thee; but before
Mayst rule it, as thou list; and poure the shame,
Which it would poure on thee, upon the floore.
  It is most just to throw that on the gound,
  Which would throw me there, if I keep the round.

6

He that is drunken, may his mother kill
Bigge with his sister: he hath lost the reins,
Is outlawd by himself: all kinde of ill
Did with his liquour slide into his veins.
  The drunkard forfets Man, and doth devest
  All worldly right, save what he hath by beast.

7

Shall I, to please anothers wine-sprung minde,
Lose all mine own? God hath giv'n me a measure
Short of his canne and bodie; must I finde
A pain in that, wherein he findes a pleasure?
  Stay at the third glasse: if thou lose thy hold,
  Then thou art modest, and the wine grows bold.

8

If reason move not Gallants, quit the room,
(All in a shipwrack shift their severall way)
Let not a common ruine thee intombe:
Be not a beast in courtesie; but stay,
 Stay at the third cup, or forgo the place.
 Wine above all things doth Gods stamp deface.

9

Yet, if thou sinne in wine or wantonnesse,
Boast not thereof; nor make thy shame thy glorie.
Frailtie gets pardon by submissivenesse;
But he that boasts, shuts that out of his storie.
 He makes flat warre with God, and doth defie
 With his poore clod of earth the spacious sky.

10

Take not his name, who made thy mouth, in vain:
It gets thee nothing, and hath no excuse.
Lust and wine plead a pleasure, avarice gain:
But the cheap swearer through his open sluce
 Lets his soul runne for nought, as little fearing.
 Were I an *Epicure*, I could bate swearing.

11

When thou dost tell anothers jest, therein
Omit the oathes, which true wit cannot need:
Pick out of tales the mirth, but not the sinne.
He pares his apple, that will cleanly feed.
 Play not away the vertue of that name,
 Which is thy best stake, when griefs make thee tame.

12

The cheapest sinnes most dearely punisht are;
Because to shun them also is so cheap:
For we have wit to mark them, and to spare.
O crumble not away thy souls fair heap.
    If thou wilt die, the gates of hell are broad:
    Pride and full sinnes have made the way a road.

13

Lie not; but let thy heart be true to God,
Thy mouth to it, thy actions to them both:
Cowards tell lies, and those that fear the rod;
The stormie working soul spits lies and froth.
    Dare to be true. Nothing can need a ly:
    A fault, which needs it most, grows two thereby.

14

Flie idlenesse, which yet thou canst not flie
By dressing, mistressing, and complement.
If those take up thy day, the sunne will crie
Against thee: for his light was onely lent.
    God gave thy soul brave wings; put not those feathers
    Into a bed, to sleep out all ill weathers.

15

Art thou a Magistrate? then be severe:
If studious, copie fair, what time hath blurr'd;
Redeem truth from his jawes: if souldier,
Chase brave employments with a naked sword
    Throughout the world. Fool not: for all may have,
    If they dare try, a glorious life, or grave.

16

O England! full of sinne, but most of sloth;
Spit out thy flegme, and fill thy brest with glorie:
Thy Gentrie bleats, as if thy native cloth
Transfus'd a sheepishnesse into thy storie:
   Not that they all are so; but that the most
   Are gone to grasse, and in the pasture lost.

17

This losse springs chiefly from our education.
Some till their ground, but let weeds choke their sonne:
Some mark a partridge, never their childes fashion:
Some ship them over, and the thing is done.
   Studie this art, make it thy great designe;
   And if Gods image move thee not, let thine.

18

Some great estates provide, but doe not breed
A mast'ring minde; so both are lost thereby:
Or els they breed them tender, make them need
All that they leave: this is flat povertie.
   For he, that needs five thousand pound to live,
   Is full as poore as he, that needs but five.

19

The way to make thy sonne rich is to fill
His minde with rest, before his trunk with riches:
For wealth without contentment climbes a hill
To feel those tempests, which fly over ditches.
   But if thy sonne can make ten pound his measure,
   Then all thou addest may be call'd his treasure.

20

When thou dost purpose ought within thy power,
Be sure to doe it, though it be but small:
Constancie knits the bones, and makes us stowre,
When wanton pleasures becken us to thrall.
    Who breaks his own bond, forfeiteth himself:
    What nature made a ship, he makes a shelf.

21

Doe all things like a man, not sneakingly:
Think the king sees thee still; for his King does.
Simpring is but a lay-hypocrisie:
Give it a corner, and the clue undoes.
    Who fears to do ill, sets himself to task:
    Who fears to do well, sure should wear a mask.

22

Look to thy mouth; diseases enter there.
Thou hast two sconses, if thy stomack call;
Carve, or discourse; do not a famine fear.
Who carves, is kind to two; who talks, to all.
    Look on meat, think it dirt, then eat a bit;
    And say withall, Earth to earth I commit.

23

Slight those who say amidst their sickly healths,
Thou liv'st by rule. What doth not so, but man?
Houses are built by rule, and common-wealths.
Entice the trusty sunne, if that thou can,
    From his Ecliptick line: becken the skie.
    Who lives by rule then, keeps good companie.

24

Who keeps no guard upon himself, is slack,
And rots to nothing at the next great thaw.
Man is a shop of rules, a well truss'd pack,
Whose every parcell under-writes a law.
    Lose not thy self, nor give thy humours way:
    God gave them to thee under lock and key.

25

By all means use sometimes to be alone.
Salute thy self: see what thy soul doth wear.
Dare to look in thy chest, for 'tis thine own:
And tumble up and down what thou find'st there.
    Who cannot rest till hee good-fellows finde,
    He breaks up house, turns out of doores his minde.

26

Be thriftie, but not covetous: therefore give
Thy need, thine honour, and thy friend his due.
Never was scraper brave man. Get to live;
Then live, and use it: els, it is not true
    That thou hast gotten. Surely use alone
    Makes money not a contemptible stone.

27

Never exceed thy income. Youth may make
Ev'n with the yeare: but age, if it will hit,
Shoots a bow short, and lessens still his stake,
As the day lessens, and his life with it.
    Thy children, kindred, friends upon thee call;
    Before thy journey fairly part with all.

28

Yet in thy thriving still misdoubt some evil;
Lest gaining gain on thee, and make thee dimme
To all things els. Wealth is the conjurers devil;
Whom when he thinks he hath, the devil hath him.
  Gold thou mayst safely touch; but if it stick
  Unto thy hands, it woundeth to the quick.

29

What skills it, if a bag of stones or gold
About thy neck do drown thee? raise thy head;
Take starres for money; starres not to be told
By any art, yet to be purchased.
  None is so wastefull as the scraping dame.
  She loseth three for one; her soul, rest, fame.

30

By no means runne in debt: take thine own measure.
Who cannot live on twentie pound a yeare,
Cannot on fourtie: he's a man of pleasure,
A kinde of thing that's for it self too deere.
  The curious unthrift makes his clothes too wide,
  And spares himself, but would his taylor chide.

31

Spend not on hopes. They that by pleading clothes
Do fortunes seek, when worth and service fail,
Would have their tale beleeved for their oathes,
And are like empty vessels under sail.
  Old courtiers know this; therefore set out so,
  As all the day thou mayst hold out to go.

32

In clothes, cheap handsomnesse doth bear the bell.
Wisedome's a trimmer thing then shop e're gave.
Say not then, This with that lace will do well;
But, This with my discretion will be brave.
  Much curiousnesse is a perpetuall wooing,
  Nothing with labour, folly long a-doing.

33

Play not for gain, but sport. Who playes for more
Then he can lose with pleasure, stakes his heart;
Perhaps his wives too, and whom she hath bore:
Servants and churches also play their part.
  Onely a herauld, who that way doth passe,
  Findes his crackt name at length in the church-glasse.

34

If yet thou love game at so deere a rate,
Learn this, that hath old gamesters deerely cost:
Dost lose? rise up: dost winne? rise in that state.
Who strive to sit out losing hands, are lost.
  Game is a civil gunpowder, in peace
  Blowing up houses with their whole increase.

35

In conversation boldnesse now bears sway.
But know, that nothing can so foolish be,
As empty boldnesse: therefore first assay
To stuffe thy minde with solid braverie;
  Then march on gallant: get substantiall worth.
  Boldnesse guilds finely, and will set it forth.

36

Be sweet to all. Is thy complexion sowre?
Then keep such companie; make them thy allay:
Get a sharp wife, a servant that will lowre.
A stumbler stumbles least in rugged way.
    Command thy self in chief. He lifes warre knows,
    Whom all his passions follow, as he goes.

37

Catch not at quarrels. He that dares not speak
Plainly and home, is coward of the two.
Think not thy fame at ev'ry twitch will break:
By great deeds shew, that thou canst little do;
    And do them not: that shall thy wisdome be;
    And change thy temperance into braverie.

38

If that thy fame with ev'ry toy be pos'd,
'Tis a thinne webbe, which poysonous fancies make:
But the great souldiers honour was compos'd
Of thicker stuffe, which would endure a shake.
    Wisdome picks friends; civilitie playes the rest.
    A toy shunn'd cleanly passeth with the best.

39

Laugh not too much: the wittie man laughs least:
For wit is newes onely to ignorance.
Lesse at thine own things laugh; lest in the jest
Thy person share, and the conceit advance.
    Make not thy sport, abuses: for the fly
    That feeds on dung, is coloured thereby.

40

Pick out of mirth, like stones out of thy ground,
Profanenesse, filthinesse, abusivenesse.
These are the scumme, with which course wits abound:
The fine may spare these well, yet not go lesse.
   All things are bigge with jest: nothing that's plain,
   But may be wittie, if thou hast the vein.

41

Wit's an unruly engine, wildly striking
Sometimes a friend, sometimes the engineer.
Hast thou the knack? pamper it not with liking:
But if thou want it, buy it not too deere.
   Many, affecting wit beyond their power,
   Have got to be a deare fool for an houre.

42

A sad wise valour is the brave complexion,
That leads the van, and swallows up the cities.
The gigler is a milk-maid, whom infection
Or a fir'd beacon frighteth from his ditties.
   Then he's the sport: the mirth then in him rests,
   And the sad man is cock of all his jests.

43

Towards great persons use respective boldnesse:
That temper gives them theirs, and yet doth take
Nothing from thine: in service, care or coldnesse
Doth ratably thy fortunes marre or make.
   Feed no man in his sinnes: for adulation
   Doth make thee parcell-devil in damnation.

44

Envie not greatnesse: for thou mak'st thereby
Thy self the worse, and so the distance greater.
Be not thine own worm: yet such jealousie,
As hurts not others, but may make thee better,
   Is a good spurre. Correct thy passions spite;
   Then may the beasts draw thee to happy light.

45

When basenesse is exalted, do not bate
The place its honour, for the persons sake.
The shrine is that which thou dost venerate,
And not the beast, that bears it on his back.
   I care not though the cloth of state should be
   Not of rich arras, but mean tapestrie.

46

Thy friend put in thy bosome: wear his eies
Still in thy heart, that he may see what's there.
If cause require, thou art his sacrifice;
Thy drops of bloud must pay down all his fear:
   But love is lost, the way of friendship's gone,
   Though *David* had his *Jonathan*, *Christ* his *John*.

47

Yet be not surety, if thou be a father.
Love is a personall debt. I cannot give
My childrens right, nor ought he take it: rather
Both friends should die, then hinder them to live.
   Fathers first enter bonds to natures ends;
   And are her sureties, ere they are a friends.

48

If thou be single, all thy goods and ground
Submit to love; but yet not more then all.
Give one estate, as one life. None is bound
To work for two, who brought himself to thrall.
   God made me one man; love makes me no more,
   Till labour come, and make my weaknesse score.

49

In thy discourse, if thou desire to please,
All such is courteous, usefull, new, or wittie.
Usefulnesse comes by labour, wit by ease;
Courtesie grows in court; news in the citie.
   Get a good stock of these, then draw the card
   That suites him best, of whom thy speech is heard.

50

Entice all neatly to what they know best;
For so thou dost thy self and him a pleasure:
(But a proud ignorance will lose his rest,
Rather then shew his cards.) Steal from his treasure
   What to ask further. Doubts well rais'd do lock
   The speaker to thee, and preserve thy stock.

51

If thou be Master-gunner, spend not all
That thou canst speak, at once; but husband it,
And give men turns of speech: do not forestall
By lavishnesse thine own, and others wit,
   As if thou mad'st thy will. A civil guest
   Will no more talk all, then eat all the feast.

52

Be calm in arguing: for fiercenesse makes
Errour a fault, and truth discourtesie.
Why should I feel another mans mistakes
More then his sicknesses or povertie?
  In love I should: but anger is not love,
  Nor wisdome neither: therefore gently move.

53

Calmnesse is great advantage: he that lets
Another chafe, may warm him at his fire,
Mark all his wandrings, and enjoy his frets;
As cunning fencers suffer heat to tire.
  Truth dwels not in the clouds: the bow that's there
  Doth often aim at, never hit the sphere.

54

Mark what another sayes: for many are
Full of themselves, and answer their own notion.
Take all into thee; then with equall care
Ballance each dramme of reason, like a potion.
  If truth be with thy friend, be with them both:
  Share in the conquest, and confesse a troth.

55

Be usefull where thou livest, that they may
Both want and wish thy pleasing presence still.
Kindnesse, good parts, great places are the way
To compasse this. Finde out mens wants and will,
  And meet them there. All worldly joyes go lesse
  To the one joy of doing kindnesses.

56

Pitch thy behaviour low, thy projects high;
So shalt thou humble and magnanimous be:
Sink not in spirit: who aimeth at the sky,
Shoots higher much then he that means a tree.
    A grain of glorie mixt with humblenesse
    Cures both a fever and lethargicknesse.

57

Let thy minde still be bent, still plotting where,
And when, and how the businesse may be done.
Slacknesse breeds worms; but the sure traveller,
Though he alight sometimes, still goeth on.
    Active and stirring spirits live alone.
    Write on the others, Here lies such a one.

58

Slight not the smallest losse, whether it be
In love or honour: take account of all;
Shine like the sunne in every corner: see
Whether thy stock of credit swell, or fall.
    Who say, I care not, those I give for lost;
    And to instruct them, will not quit the cost.

59

Scorn no mans love, though of a mean degree;
Love is a present for a mightie king.
Much lesse make any one thy enemie.
As gunnes destroy, so may a little sling.
    The cunning workman never doth refuse
    The meanest tool, that he may chance to use.

60

All forrain wisdome doth amount to this,
To take all that is given; whether wealth,
Or love, or language; nothing comes amisse:
A good digestion turneth all to health:
    And then as farre as fair behaviour may,
    Strike off all scores; none are so cleare as they.

61

Keep all thy native good, and naturalize
All forrain of that name; but scorn their ill:
Embrace their activenesse, not vanities.
Who follows all things, forfeiteth his will.
    If thou observest strangers in each fit,
    In time they'l runne thee out of all thy wit.

62

Affect in things about thee cleanlinesse,
That all may gladly board thee, as a flowre.
Slovens take up their stock of noisomnesse
Beforehand, and anticipate their last houre.
    Let thy mindes sweetnesse have his operation
    Upon thy body, clothes, and habitation.

63

In Almes regard thy means, and others merit.
Think heav'n a better bargain, then to give
Onely thy single market-money for it.
Joyn hands with God to make a man to live.
    Give to all something; to a good poore man,
    Till thou change names, and be where he began.

64

Man is Gods image; but a poore man is
Christs stamp to boot: both images regard.
God reckons for him, counts the favour his:
Write, So much giv'n to God; thou shalt be heard.
　　Let thy almes go before, and keep heav'ns gate
　　Open for thee; or both may come too late.

65

Restore to God his due in tithe and time:
A tithe purloin'd cankers the whole estate.
Sundaies observe: think when the bells do chime,
'Tis angels musick; therefore come not late.
　　God then deals blessings: If a king did so,
　　Who would not haste, nay give, to see the show?

66

Twice on the day his due is understood;
For all the week thy food so oft he gave thee.
Thy cheere is mended; bate not of the food,
Because 'tis better, and perhaps may save thee.
　　Thwart not the Mighty God: O be not crosse.
　　Fast when thou wilt but then, 'tis gain not losse.

67

Though private prayer be a brave designe,
Yet publick hath more promises, more love:
And love's a weight to hearts, to eies a signe.
We all are but cold suitours; let us move
　　Where it is warmest. Leave thy six and seven;
　　Pray with the most: for where most pray, is heaven.

68

When once thy foot enters the church, be bare.
God is more there, then thou: for thou art there
Onely by his permission. Then beware,
And make thy self all reverence and fear.
    Kneeling ne're spoil'd silk stocking: quit thy state.
    All equal are within the churches gate.

69

Resort to sermons, but to prayers most:
Praying's the end of preaching. O be drest;
Stay not for th' other pin: why, thou hast lost
A joy for it worth worlds. Thus hell doth jest
    Away thy blessings, and extreamly flout thee,
    Thy clothes being fast, but thy soul loose about thee.

70

In time of service seal up both thine eies,
And send them to thine heart; that spying sinne,
They may weep out the stains by them did rise:
Those doores being shut, all by the eare comes in.
    Who marks in church-time others symmetrie,
    Makes all their beautie his deformitie.

71

Let vain or busie thoughts have there no part:
Bring not thy plough, thy plots, thy pleasures thither.
Christ purg'd his temple; so must thou thy heart.
All worldly thoughts are but theeves met together
    To couzin thee. Look to thy actions well:
    For churches are either our heav'n or hell.

72

Judge not the preacher; for he is thy Judge:
If thou mislike him, thou conceiv'st him not.
God calleth preaching folly. Do not grudge
To pick out treasures from an earthen pot.
The worst speak something good: if all want sense,
God takes a text, and preacheth patience.

73

He that gets patience, and the blessing which
Preachers conclude with, hath not lost his pains.
He that by being at church escapes the ditch,
Which he might fall in by companions, gains.
He that loves Gods abode, and to combine
With saints on earth, shall one day with them shine.

74

Jest not at preachers language, or expression:
How know'st thou, but thy sinnes made him miscarrie?
Then turn thy faults and his into confession:
God sent him, whatsoe're he be: O tarry,
And love him for his Master: his condition,
Though it be ill, makes him no ill Physician.

75

None shall in hell such bitter pangs endure,
As those, who mock at Gods way of salvation.
Whom oil and balsames kill, what salve can cure?
They drink with greedinesse a full damnation.
The Jews refused thunder; and we, folly.
Though God do hedge us in, yet who is holy?

76

Summe up at night, what thou hast done by day;
And in the morning, what thou hast to do.
Dresse and undresse thy soul: mark the decay
And growth of it: if with thy watch, that too
    Be down, then winde up both; since we shall be
    Most surely judg'd, make thy accounts agree.

77

In brief, acquit thee bravely; play the man.
Look not on pleasures as they come, but go.
Deferre not the least vertue: lifes poore span
Make not an ell, by trifling in thy wo.
    If thou do ill; the joy fades, not the pains:
    If well; the pain doth fade, the joy remains.

The Sacrifice

Oh all ye, who passe by, whose eyes and minde
To worldly things are sharp, but to me blinde;
To me, who took eyes that I might you finde:
                    Was ever grief like mine?

The Princes of my people make a head
Against their Maker: they do wish me dead,
Who cannot wish, except I give them bread:
                    Was ever grief like mine?

Without me each one, who doth now me brave,
Had to this day been an Egyptian slave.
They use that power against me, which I gave:
                    Was ever grief like mine?

Mine own Apostle, who the bag did beare,
Though he had all I had, did not forbeare
To sell me also, and to put me there:
                    Was ever grief like mine?

For thirtie pence he did my death devise,
Who at three hundred did the ointment prize,
Not half so sweet as my sweet sacrifice:
                    Was ever grief like mine?

Therefore my soul melts, and my hearts deare treasure
Drops bloud (the onely beads) my words to measure:
O let this cup passe, if it be thy pleasure:
                    Was ever grief like mine?

These drops being temper'd with a sinners tears
A Balsome are for both the Hemispheres:
Curing all wounds, but mine; all, but my fears:
                    Was ever grief like mine?

Yet my Disciples sleep: I cannot gain
One houre of watching; but their drowsie brain
Comforts not me, and doth my doctrine stain:
                    Was ever grief like mine?

Arise, arise, they come. Look how they runne!
Alas! what haste they make to be undone!
How with their lanterns do they seek the sunne!
                    Was ever grief like mine?

With clubs and staves they seek me, as a thief,
Who am the Way and Truth, the true relief;
Most true to those, who are my greatest grief:
                    Was ever grief like mine?

Judas, dost thou betray me with a kisse?
Canst thou finde hell about my lips? and misse
Of life, just at the gates of life and blisse?
                    Was ever grief like mine?

See, they lay hold on me, not with the hands
Of faith, but furie: yet at their commands
I suffer binding, who have loos'd their bands:
                    Was ever grief like mine?

All my Disciples flie; fear puts a barre
Betwixt my friends and me. They leave the starre,
That brought the wise men of the East from farre.
                    Was ever grief like mine?

Then from one ruler to another bound
They leade me; urging, that it was not sound
What I taught: Comments would the text confound.
                      Was ever grief like mine?

The Priest and rulers all false witnesse seek
'Gainst him, who seeks not life, but is the meek
And readie Paschal Lambe of this great week:
                      Was ever grief like mine?

Then they accuse me of great blasphemie,
That I did thrust into the Deitie,
Who never thought that any robberie:
                      Was ever grief like mine?

Some said, that I the Temple to the floore
In three dayes raz'd, and raised as before.
Why, he that built the world can do much more:
                      Was ever grief like mine?

Then they condemne me all with that same breath,
Which I do give them daily, unto death.
Thus *Adam* my first breathing rendereth:
                      Was ever grief like mine?

They binde, and leade me unto *Herod :* he
Sends me to *Pilate*. This makes them agree;
But yet their friendship is my enmitie:
                      Was ever grief like mine?

Herod and all his bands do set me light,
Who teach all hands to warre, fingers to fight,
And onely am the Lord of Hosts and might:
                      Was ever grief like mine?

Herod in judgement sits, while I do stand;
Examines me with a censorious hand:
I him obey, who all things else command:
                                    Was ever grief like mine?

The *Jews* accuse me with despitefulnesse;
And vying malice with my gentlenesse,
Pick quarrels with their onely happinesse:
                                    Was ever grief like mine?

I answer nothing, but with patience prove
If stonie hearts will melt with gentle love.
But who does hawk at eagles with a dove?
                                    Was ever grief like mine?

My silence rather doth augment their crie;
My dove doth back into my bosome flie,
Because the raging waters still are high:
                                    Was ever grief like mine?

Heark how they crie aloud still, *Crucifie*:
It is not fit he live a day, they crie,
Who cannot live lesse then eternally:
                                    Was ever grief like mine?

Pilate, a stranger, holdeth off; but they,
Mine owne deare people, cry, *Away, Away*,
With noises confused frighting the day:
                                    Was ever grief like mine?

Yet still they shout, and crie, and stop their eares,
Putting my life among their sinnes and feares,
And therefore wish *my bloud on them and theirs*:
                                    Was ever grief like mine?

See how spite cankers things. These words aright
Used, and wished, are the whole worlds light:
But hony is their gall, brightnesse their night:
                 Was ever grief like mine?

They choose a murderer, and all agree
In him to do themselves a courtesie:
For it was their own case who killed me:
                 Was ever grief like mine?

And a seditious murderer he was:
But I the Prince of peace; peace that doth passe
All understanding, more then heav'n doth glasse:
                 Was ever grief like mine?

Why, Caesar is their onely King, not I:
He clave the stonie rock, when they were drie;
But surely not their hearts, as I well trie:
                 Was ever grief like mine?

Ah! how they scourge me! yet my tendernesse
Doubles each lash: and yet their bitternesse
Windes up my grief to a mysteriousnesse:
                 Was ever grief like mine?

They buffet him, and box him as they list,
Who grasps the earth and heaven with his fist,
And never yet, whom he would punish, miss'd:
                 Was ever grief like mine?

Behold, they spit on me in scornfull wise,
Who by my spittle gave the blinde man eies,
Leaving his blindnesse to my enemies:
                 Was ever grief like mine?

My face they cover, though it be divine.
As *Moses* face was vailed, so is mine
Lest on their double-dark souls either shine:
                     Was ever grief like mine?

Servants and abjects flout me; they are wittie:
Now prophesie who strikes thee, is their dittie.
So they in me denie themselves all pitie:
                     Was ever grief like mine?

And now I am deliver'd unto death,
Which each one calls for so with utmost breath,
That he before me well nigh suffereth:
                     Was ever grief like mine?

Weep not, deare friends, since I for both have wept
When all my tears were bloud, the while you slept:
Your tears for your own fortunes should be kept:
                     Was ever grief like mine?

The souldiers lead me to the Common Hall;
There they deride me, they abuse me all:
Yet for twelve heav'nly legions I could call:
                     Was ever grief like mine?

Then with a scarlet robe they me aray;
Which shews my bloud to be the onely way
And cordiall left to repair mans decay:
                     Was ever grief like mine?

Then on my head a crown of thorns I wear:
For these are all the grapes *Sion* doth bear,
Though I my vine planted and watred there:
                     Was ever grief like mine?

So sits the earths great curse in *Adams* fall
Upon my head: so I remove it all
From th' earth unto my brows, and bear the thrall:
>   Was ever grief like mine?

Then with the reed they gave to me before,
They strike my head, the rock from whence all store
Of heav'nly blessings issue evermore:
>   Was ever grief like mine?

They bow their knees to me, and cry, *Hail king:*
What ever scoffes & scornfulness can bring,
I am the floore, the sink, where they it fling:
>   Was ever grief like mine?

Yet since mans scepters are as frail as reeds,
And thorny all their crowns, bloudie their weeds;
I, who am Truth, turn into truth their deeds:
>   Was ever grief like mine?

The souldiers also spit upon that face,
Which Angels did desire to have the grace,
And Prophets, once to see, but found no place:
>   Was ever grief like mine?

Thus trimmed, forth they bring me to the rout,
Who *Crucifie him*, crie with one strong shout.
God holds his peace at man, and man cries out:
>   Was ever grief like mine?

They leade me in once more, and putting then
Mine own clothes on, they leade me out agen.
Whom devils flie, thus is he toss'd of men:
>   Was ever grief like mine?

And now wearie of sport, glad to ingrosse
All spite in one, counting my life their losse,
They carrie me to my most bitter crosse:
>   Was ever grief like mine?

My crosse I bear my self, untill I faint:
Then Simon bears it for me by constraint,
The decreed burden of each mortall Saint:
>   Was ever grief like mine?

O all ye who passe by, behold and see;
Man stole the fruit, but I must climbe the tree;
The tree of life to all, but onely me:
>   Was ever grief like mine?

Lo, here I hang, charg'd with a world of sinne,
The greater world o' th' two; for that came in
By words, but this by sorrow I must win:
>   Was ever grief like mine?

Such sorrow as, if sinfull man could feel,
Or feel his part, he would not cease to kneel,
Till all were melted, though he were all steel:
>   Was ever grief like mine?

But, *O my God, my God!* why leav'st thou me,
The sonne, in whom thou dost delight to be ?
My God, my God –
>   Never was grief like mine.

Shame tears my soul, my bodie many a wound;
Sharp nails pierce this, but sharper that confound;
Reproches, which are free, while I am bound.
>   Was ever grief like mine?

Now heal thy self, Physician; now come down.
Alas! I did so, when I left my crown
And fathers smile for you, to feel his frown:
Was ever grief like mine?

In healing not my self, there doth consist
All that salvation, which ye now resist;
Your safetie in my sicknesse doth subsist:
Was ever grief like mine?

Betwixt two theeves I spend my utmost breath,
As he that for some robberie suffereth.
Alas! what have I stollen from you? Death.
Was ever grief like mine?

A king my title is, prefixt on high;
Yet by my subjects am condemn'd to die
A servile death in servile companie:
Was ever grief like mine?

They give me vineger mingled with gall,
But more with malice: yet, when they did call,
With Manna, Angels food, I fed them all:
Was ever grief like mine?

They part my garments, and by lot dispose
My coat, the type of love, which once cur'd those
Who sought for help, never malicious foes:
Was ever grief like mine?

Nay, after death their spite shall further go;
For they will pierce my side, I full well know;
That as sinne came, so Sacraments might flow:
Was ever grief like mine?

But now I die; now all is finished.
My wo, mans weal: and now I bow my head.
Onely let others say, when I am dead,
                    Never was grief like mine.

The Reprisall

I have consider'd it, and finde
There is no dealing with thy mighty passion:
For though I die for thee, I am behinde;
   My sinnes deserve the condemnation.

O make me innocent, that I
May give a disentangled state and free:
And yet thy wounds still my attempts defie,
   For by thy death I die for thee.

Ah! was it not enough that thou
By thy eternall glorie didst outgo me?
Couldst thou not griefs sad conquests me allow,
   But in all vict'ries overthrow me?

Yet by confession will I come
Into thy conquest: though I can do nought
Against thee, in thee I will overcome
   The man, who once against thee fought.

The Sinner

Lord, how I am all ague, when I seek
  What I have treasur'd in my memorie!
  Since, if my soul make even with the week,
Each seventh note by right is due to thee.
I finde there quarries of pil'd vanities,
  But shreds of holinesse, that dare not venture
  'To shew their face, since crosse to thy decrees:
There the circumference earth is, heav'n the centre.
In so much dregs the quintessence is small:
  The spirit and good extract of my heart
  Comes to about the many hundred part.
Yet Lord restore thine image, heare my call:
  And though my hard heart scarce to thee can grone,
  Remember that thou once didst write in stone.

Redemption

Having been tenant long to a rich Lord,
    Not thriving, I resolved to be bold,
    And make a suit unto him, to afford
A new small-rented lease, and cancell th' old.
In heaven at his manour I him sought:
    They told me there, that he was lately gone
    About some land, which he had dearly bought
Long since on earth, to take possession.
I straight return'd, and knowing his great birth,
    Sought him accordingly in great resorts;
    In cities, theatres, gardens, parks, and courts:
At length I heard a ragged noise and mirth
    Of theeves and murderers: there I him espied,
    Who straight, *Your suit is granted*, said, & died.

Easter-Wings

Lord, who createdst man in wealth and store,
    Though foolishly he lost the same,
        Decaying more and more,
            Till he became
             Most poore:
             With thee
            O let me rise
        As larks, harmoniously,
    And sing this day thy victories:
Then shall the fall further the flight in me.

My tender age in sorrow did beginne:
    And still with sicknesses and shame
        Thou didst so punish sinne,
            That I became
             Most thinne.
             With thee
            Let me combine
        And feel this day thy victorie:
    For, if I imp my wing on thine,
Affliction shall advance the flight in me.

Nature

Full of rebellion, I would die,
Or fight, or travell, or denie
That thou hast ought to do with me.
                    O tame my heart;
                    It is thy highest art
To captivate strong holds to thee.

If thou shalt let this venome lurk,
And in suggestions fume and work,
My soul will turn to bubbles straight,
                    And thence by kinde
                    Vanish into a winde,
Making thy workmanship deceit.

O smooth my rugged heart, and there
Engrave thy rev'rend Law and fear;
Or make a new one, since the old
                    Is saplesse grown,
                    And a much fitter stone
To hide my dust, then thee to hold.

Sinne

Lord, with what care hast thou begirt us round!
  Parents first season us: then schoolmasters
  Deliver us to laws; they send us bound
To rules of reason, holy messengers,
Pulpits and Sundayes, sorrow dogging sinne,
  Afflictions sorted, anguish of all sizes,
  Fine nets and stratagems to catch us in,
Bibles laid open, millions of surprises,
Blessings beforehand, tyes of gratefulnesse,
  The sound of glorie ringing in our eares:
  Without, our shame; within, our consciences;
Angels and grace, eternall hopes and fears.
  Yet all these fences and their whole aray
  One cunning bosome-sinne blows quite away.

Affliction

When first thou didst entice to thee my heart,
                     I thought the service brave:
So many joyes I writ down for my part,
                     Besides what I might have
Out of my stock of naturall delights,
Augmented with thy gracious benefits.

I looked on thy furniture so fine,
                     And made it fine to me:
Thy glorious houshold-stuffe did me entwine,
                     And 'tice me unto thee.
Such starres I counted mine: both heav'n and earth
Payd me my wages in a world of mirth.

What pleasures could I want, whose King I served,
                     Where joyes my fellows were?
Thus argu'd into hopes, my thoughts reserved
                     No place for grief or fear.
Therefore my sudden soul caught at the place,
And made her youth and fiercenesse seek thy face.

At first thou gav'st me milk and sweetnesses;
                     I had my wish and way:
My dayes were straw'd with flow'rs and happinesse;
                     There was no moneth but May.
But with my yeares sorrow did twist and grow,
And made a partie unawares for wo.

My flesh began unto my soul in pain,
               Sicknesses cleave my bones;
Consuming agues dwell in ev'ry vein,
               And tune my breath to grones.
Sorrow was all my soul; I scarce beleeved,
Till grief did tell me roundly, that I lived.

When I got health, thou took'st away my life,
               And more; for my friends die:
My mirth and edge was lost; a blunted knife
               Was of more use then I.
Thus thinne and lean without a fence or friend,
I was blown through with ev'ry storm and winde.

Whereas my birth and spirit rather took
               The way that takes the town;
Thou didst betray me to a lingring book,
               And wrap me in a gown.
I was entangled in the world of strife,
Before I had the power to change my life.

Yet, for I threatned oft the siege to raise,
               Not simpring all mine age,
Thou often didst with Academick praise
               Melt and dissolve my rage.
I took thy sweetned pill, till I came where
I could not go away, nor persevere.

Yet lest perchance I should too happie be
               In my unhappinesse,
Turning my purge to food, thou throwest me
               Into more sicknesses.
Thus doth thy power crosse-bias me, not making
Thine own gift good, yet me from my wayes taking.

Now I am here, what thou wilt do with me
                None of my books will show:
I reade, and sigh, and wish I were a tree;
                For sure then I should grow
To fruit or shade: at least some bird would trust
Her houshold to me, and I should be just.

Yet, though thou troublest me, I must be meek;
                In weaknesse must be stout.
Well, I will change the service, and go seek
                Some other master out.
Ah my deare God! though I am clean forgot,
Let me not love thee, if I love thee not.

Prayer

Prayer the Churches banquet, Angels age,
    Gods breath in man returning to his birth,
    The soul in paraphrase, heart in pilgrimage,
The Christian plummet sounding heav'n and earth;
Engine against th' Almightie, sinners towre,
    Reversed thunder, Christ-side-piercing spear,
    The six-daies world transposing in an houre,
A kind of tune, which all things heare and fear;
Softnesse, and peace, and joy, and love, and blisse,
    Exalted Manna, gladnesse of the best,
    Heaven in ordinarie, man well drest,
The milkie way, the bird of Paradise,
    Church-bels beyond the starres heard, the souls bloud,
    The land of spices; something understood.

The Temper

How should I praise thee, Lord! how should my rymes
    Gladly engrave thy love in steel,
    If what my soul doth feel sometimes,
        My soul might ever feel!

Although there were some fourtie heav'ns, or more,
    Sometimes I peere above them all;
    Sometimes I hardly reach a score,
        Sometimes to hell I fall.

O rack me not to such a vast extent;
    Those distances belong to thee:
    The world's too little for thy tent,
        A grave too big for me.

Wilt thou meet arms with man, that thou dost stretch
    A crumme of dust from heav'n to hell?
    Will great God measure with a wretch?
        Shall he thy stature spell?

O let me, when thy roof my soul hath hid,
    O let me roost and nestle there:
    Then of a sinner thou art rid,
        And I of hope and fear.

Yet take thy way; for sure thy way is best:
    Stretch or contract me, thy poore debter:
    This is but tuning of my breast,
        To make the musick better.

Whether I flie with angels, fall with dust,
  Thy hands made both, and I am there:
  Thy power and love, my love and trust
  Make one place ev'ry where.

Jordan

Who sayes that fictions onely and false hair
Become a verse? Is there in truth no beautie?
Is all good structure in a winding stair?
May no lines passe, except they do their dutie
　　Not to a true, but painted chair?

Is it no verse, except enchanted groves
And sudden arbours shadow course-spunne lines?
Must purling streams refresh a lovers loves?
Must all be vail'd, while he that reades, divines,
　　Catching the sense at two removes?

Shepherds are honest people; let them sing:
Riddle who list, for me, and pull for Prime:
I envie no mans nightingale or spring;
Nor let them punish me with losse of rime,
　　Who plainly say, *My God*, *My King*.

Employment

If as a flowre doth spread and die,
　Thou wouldst extend me to some good,
Before I were by frosts extremitie
　　　　　Nipt in the bud;

The sweetnesse and the praise were thine;
　But the extension and the room,
Which in thy garland I should fill, were mine
　　　　　At thy great doom.

For as thou dost impart thy grace,
　The greater shall our glorie be.
The measure of our joyes is in this place,
　　　　　The stuffe with thee.

Let me not languish then, and spend
　A life as barren to thy praise,
As is the dust, to which that life doth tend,
　　　　　But with delaies.

All things are busie; onely I
　Neither bring hony with the bees,
Nor flowres to make that, nor the husbandrie
　　　　　To water these.

I am no link of thy great chain,
　But all my companie is a weed.
Lord place me in thy consort; give one strain
　　　　　To my poore reed.

Praise

To write a verse or two is all the praise,
                That I can raise:
        Mend my estate in any wayes,
                Thou shalt have more.

I go to Church; help me to wings, and I
                Will thither flie;
        Or, if I mount unto the skie,
                I will do more.

Man is all weaknesse; there is no such thing
                As Prince or King:
        His arm is short; yet with a sling
                He may do more.

An herb destill'd, and drunk, may dwell next doore,
                On the same floore,
        To a brave soul: exalt the poore,
                They can do more.

O raise me then! Poore bees, that work all day,
                Sting my delay,
        Who have a work, as well as they,
                And much, much more.

The Church-Floore

Mark you the floore? that square & speckled stone,
                    Which looks so firm and strong,
                              Is *Patience*:

And th' other black and grave, wherewith each one
                    Is checker'd all along,
                              Humilitie:

The gentle rising, which on either hand
                    Leads to the Quire above,
                              Is *Confidence*:

But the sweet cement, which in one sure band
                    Ties the whole frame, is *Love*
                              And *Charitie*.

          Hither sometimes Sinne steals, and stains
          The marbles neat and curious veins:
But all is cleansed when the marble weeps.
          Sometimes Death, puffing at the doore,
          Blows all the dust about the floore:
But while he thinks to spoil the room, he sweeps.
          Blest be the *Architect*, whose art
          Could build so strong in a weak heart.

The Windows

Lord, how can man preach thy eternall word?
   He is a brittle crazie glasse:
Yet in thy temple thou dost him afford
    This glorious and transcendent place,
    To be a window, through thy grace.

But when thou dost anneal in glasse thy storie,
    Making thy life to shine within
The holy Preachers; then the light and glorie
    More rev'rend grows, & more doth win:
    Which else shows watrish, bleak, & thin.

Doctrine and life, colours and light, in one
    When they combine and mingle, bring
A strong regard and aw: but speech alone
    Doth vanish like a flaring thing,
    And in the eare, not conscience ring.

The Quidditie

My God, a verse is not a crown,
No point of honour, or gay suit,
No hawk, or banquet, or renown,
Nor a good sword, nor yet a lute:

It cannot vault, or dance, or play;
It never was in *France* or *Spain*;
Nor can it entertain the day
With my great stable or demain:

It is no office, art, or news,
Nor the Exchange, or busie Hall;
But it is that which while I use
I am with thee, and *most take all*.

Humilitie

I saw the Vertues sitting hand in hand
In sev'rall ranks upon an azure throne,
Where all the beasts and fowl by their command
Presented tokens of submission.
Humilitie, who sat the lowest there
                            To execute their call,
When by the beasts the presents tendred were,
                            Gave them about to all.

The angrie Lion did present his paw,
Which by consent was giv'n to Mansuetude.
The fearfull Hare her eares, which by their law
Humilitie did reach to Fortitude.
The jealous Turkie brought his corall-chain;
                            That went to Temperance.
On Justice was bestow'd the Foxes brain,
                            Kill'd in the way by chance.

At length the Crow bringing the Peacocks plume,
(For he would not) as they beheld the grace
Of that brave gift, each one began to fume,
And challenge it, as proper to his place,
Till they fell out: which when the beasts espied,
                            They leapt upon the throne;
And if the Fox had liv'd to rule their side,
                            They had depos'd each one.

Humilitie, who held the plume, at this
Did weep so fast, that the tears trickling down
Spoil'd all the train: then saying, *Here it is
For which ye wrangle*, made them turn their frown

Against the beasts: so joyntly bandying,
                They drive them soon away;
And then amerc'd them, double gifts to bring
                At the next Session-day.

Employment

He that is weary, let him sit.
               My soul would stirre
And trade in courtesies and wit,
               Quitting the furre
To cold complexions needing it.

Man is no starre, but a quick coal
               Of mortall fire:
Who blows it not, nor doth controll
               A faint desire,
Lets his own ashes choke his soul.

When th' elements did for place contest
               With him, whose will
Ordain'd the highest to be best;
               The earth sat still,
And by the others is opprest.

Life is a businesse, not good cheer;
               Ever in warres.
The sunne still shineth there or here,
               Whereas the starres
Watch an advantage to appeare.

Oh that I were an Orenge-tree,
               That busie plant!
Then should I ever laden be,
               And never want
Some fruit for him that dressed me.

But we are still too young or old;
        The Man is gone,
Before we do our wares unfold:
        So we freeze on,
Untill the grave increase our cold.

Deniall

When my devotions could not pierce
                  Thy silent eares;
Then was my heart broken, as was my verse:
      My breast was full of fears
              And disorder:

My bent thoughts, like a brittle bow,
                Did flie asunder:
Each took his way; some would to pleasures go,
      Some to the warres and thunder
            Of alarms.

As good go any where, they say,
              As to benumme
Both knees and heart, in crying night and day,
      Come, come, my God, O come,
           But no hearing.

O that thou shouldst give dust a tongue
            To crie to thee,
And then not heare it crying! all day long
      My heart was in my knee,
           But no hearing.

Therefore my soul lay out of sight,
           Untun'd, unstrung:
My feeble spirit, unable to look right,
      Like a nipt blossome, hung
          Discontented.

O cheer and tune my heartlesse breast,
    Deferre no time;
That so thy favours granting my request,
    They and my minde may chime,
      And mend my ryme.

Ungratefulnesse

Lord, with what bountie and rare clemencie
        Hast thou redeem'd us from the grave!
        If thou hadst let us runne,
        Gladly had man ador'd the sunne,
          And thought his god most brave;
Where now we shall be better gods then he.

Thou hast but two rare cabinets full of treasure,
        The *Trinitie*, and *Incarnation*:
          Thou hast unlockt them both,
        And made them jewels to betroth
          The work of thy creation
Unto thy self in everlasting pleasure.

The statelier cabinet is the *Trinitie*,
        Whose sparkling light accesse denies:
          Therefore thou dost not show
        This fully to us, till death blow
          The dust into our eyes:
For by that powder thou wilt make us see.

But all thy sweets are packt up in the other;
        Thy mercies thither flock and flow:
          That as the first affrights,
        This may allure us with delights;
          Because this box we know;
For we have all of us just such another.

But man is close, reserv'd, and dark to thee:
      When thou demandest but a heart,
        He cavils instantly.
     In his poore cabinet of bone
        Sinnes have their box apart,
Defrauding thee, who gavest two for one.

Sighs and Grones

O do not use me
After my sinnes! look not on my desert,
But on thy glorie! then thou wilt reform
And not refuse me: for thou onely art
The mightie God, but I a sillie worm;
              O do not bruise me!

O do not urge me!
For what account can thy ill steward make?
I have abus'd thy stock, destroy'd thy woods,
Suckt all thy magazens: my head did ake,
Till it found out how to consume thy goods:
              O do not scourge me!

O do not blinde me!
I have deserv'd that an Egyptian night
Should thicken all my powers; because my lust
Hath still sow'd fig-leaves to exclude thy light:
But I am frailtie, and already dust;
              O do not grinde me!

O do not fill me
With the turn'd viall of thy bitter wrath!
For thou hast other vessels full of bloud,
A part whereof my Saviour empti'd hath,
Ev'n unto death: since he di'd for my good,
              O do not kill me!

            But O reprieve me!
For thou hast life and death at thy command;
Thou art both *Judge* and *Saviour*, *feast* and *rod*,
Cordiall and *Corrosive*: put not thy hand
Into the bitter box; but O my God,
            My God, relieve me!

The World

Love built a stately house; where *Fortune* came,
And spinning phansies, she was heard to say,
That her fine cobwebs did support the frame,
Whereas they were supported by the same:
But *Wisdome* quickly swept them all away.

Then *Pleasure* came, who, liking not the fashion,
Began to make *Balcones*, *Terraces*,
Till she had weakned all by alteration:
But rev'rend *laws*, and many a *proclamation*
Reformed all at length with menaces.

Then enter'd *Sinne*, and with that Sycomore,
Whose leaves first sheltred man from drought & dew,
Working and winding slily evermore,
The inward walls and sommers cleft and tore:
But *Grace* shor'd these, and cut that as it grew.

Then *Sinne* combin'd with *Death* in a firm band
To raze the building to the very floore:
Which they effected, none could them withstand.
But *Love* and *Grace* took *Glorie* by the hand,
And built a braver Palace then before.

Vanitie

The fleet Astronomer can bore,
And thred the spheres with his quick-piercing minde:
He views their stations, walks from doore to doore,
    Surveys, as if he had design'd
To make a purchase there: he sees their dances,
      And knoweth long before
Both their full-ey'd aspects, and secret glances.

The nimble Diver with his side
Cuts through the working waves, that he may fetch
His dearely-earned pearl, which God did hide
    On purpose from the ventrous wretch;
That he might save his life, and also hers,
      Who with excessive pride
Her own destruction and his danger wears.

The subtil Chymick can devest
And strip the creature naked, till he finde
The callow principles within their nest:
    There he imparts to them his minde,
Admitted to their bed-chamber, before
      They appeare trim and drest
To ordinarie suitours at the doore.

What hath not man sought out and found,
But his deare God? who yet his glorious law
Embosomes in us, mellowing the ground
    With showres and frosts, with love & aw,
So that we need not say, Where's this command?
      Poore man, thou searchest round
To finde out *death*, but missest *life* at hand.

Vertue

Sweet day, so cool, so calm, so bright,
The bridall of the earth and skie:
The dew shall weep thy fall to night;
            For thou must die.

Sweet rose, whose hue angrie and brave
Bids the rash gazer wipe his eye:
Thy root is ever in its grave,
            And thou must die.

Sweet spring, full of sweet dayes and roses,
A box where sweets compacted lie;
My musick shows ye have your closes,
            And all must die.

Onely a sweet and vertuous soul,
Like season'd timber, never gives;
But though the whole world turn to coal,
            Then chiefly lives.

The Pearl

I know the wayes of Learning; both the head
And pipes that feed the presse, and make it runne;
What reason hath from nature borrowed,
Or of it self, like a good huswife, spunne
In laws and policie; what the starres conspire,
What willing nature speaks, what forc'd by fire;
Both th' old discoveries, and the new-found seas,
The stock and surplus, cause and historie:
All these stand open, or I have the keyes:
                Yet I love thee.

I know the wayes of Honour, what maintains
The quick returns of courtesie and wit:
In vies of favours whether partie gains,
When glorie swells the heart, and moldeth it
To all expressions both of hand and eye,
Which on the world a true-love-knot may tie,
And bear the bundle, wheresoe're it goes:
How many drammes of spirit there must be
To sell my life unto my friends or foes:
                Yet I love thee.

I know the wayes of Pleasure, the sweet strains,
The lullings and the relishes of it;
The propositions of hot bloud and brains;
What mirth and musick mean; what love and wit
Have done these twentie hundred yeares, and more:
I know the projects of unbridled store:
My stuffe is flesh, not brasse; my senses live,
And grumble oft, that they have more in me
Then he that curbs them, being but one to five:
                Yet I love thee.

I know all these, and have them in my hand:
Therefore not sealed, but with open eyes
I flie to thee, and fully understand
Both the main sale, and the commodities;
And at what rate and price I have thy love;
With all the circumstances that may move:
Yet through these labyrinths, not my groveling wit,
But thy silk twist let down from heav'n to me,
Did both conduct and teach me, how by it
                To climbe to thee.

Man

My God, I heard this day,
That none doth build a stately habitation,
But he that means to dwell therein.
What house more stately hath there been,
Or can be, then is Man? to whose creation
All things are in decay.

For Man is ev'ry thing,
And more: He is a tree, yet bears more fruit;
A beast, yet is, or should be more:
Reason and speech we onely bring.
Parrats may thank us, if they are not mute,
They go upon the score.

Man is all symmetrie,
Full of proportions, one limbe to another,
And all to all the world besides:
Each part may call the furthest, brother:
For head with foot hath private amitie,
And both with moons and tides.

Nothing hath got so farre,
But Man hath caught and kept it, as his prey.
His eyes dismount the highest starre:
He is in little all the sphere.
Herbs gladly cure our flesh; because that they
Finde their acquaintance there.

For us the windes do blow,
The earth doth rest, heav'n move, and fountains flow.
Nothing we see, but means our good,
As our delight, or as our treasure:

The whole is, either our cupboard of food,
   Or cabinet of pleasure.

   The starres have us to bed;
Night draws the curtain, which the sunne withdraws;
   Musick and light attend our head.
   All things unto our flesh are kinde
In their descent and being; to our minde
   In their ascent and cause.

   Each thing is full of dutie:
Waters united are our navigation;
   Distinguished, our habitation;
   Below, our drink; above, our meat;
Both are our cleanlinesse. Hath one such beautie?
   Then how are all things neat?

   More servants wait on Man,
Then he'l take notice of: in ev'ry path
   He treads down that which doth befriend him,
   When sicknesse makes him pale and wan.
Oh mightie love! Man is one world, and hath
   Another to attend him.

   Since then, my God, thou hast
So brave a Palace built; O dwell in it,
   That it may dwell with thee at last!
   Till then, afford us so much wit;
That, as the world serves us, we may serve thee,
   And both thy servants be.

Charms and Knots

Who reade a chapter when they rise,
Shall ne're be troubled with ill eyes.

A poore mans rod, when thou dost ride,
Is both a weapon and a guide.

Who shuts his hand, hath lost his gold:
Who opens it, hath it twice told.

Who goes to bed and does not pray,
Maketh two nights to ev'ry day.

Who by aspersions throw a stone
At th' head of others, hit their own.

Who looks on ground with humble eyes,
Findes himself there, and seeks to rise.

When th' hair is sweet through pride or lust,
The powder doth forget the dust.

Take one from ten, and what remains?
Ten still, if sermons go for gains.

In shallow waters heav'n doth show;
But who drinks on, to hell may go.

Miserie

Lord, let the Angels praise thy name.
Man is a foolish thing, a foolish thing,
    Folly and Sinne play all his game.
His house still burns, and yet he still doth sing,
        Man is but grasse,
        He knows it, fill the glasse.

How canst thou brook his foolishnesse?
Why, he'l not lose a cup of drink for thee:
    Bid him but temper his excesse;
Not he: he knows where he can better be,
        As he will swear,
        Then to serve thee in fear.

What strange pollutions doth he wed,
And make his own? as if none knew but he.
    No man shall beat into his head,
That thou within his curtains drawn canst see:
        They are of cloth,
        Where never yet came moth.

The best of men, turn but thy hand
For one poore minute, stumble at a pinne:
    They would not have their actions scann'd,
Nor any sorrow tell them that they sinne,
        Though it be small,
        And measure not their fall.

They quarrell thee, and would give over
The bargain made to serve thee: but thy love
   Holds them unto it, and doth cover
Their follies with the wing of thy milde Dove,
        Not suff'ring those
        Who would, to be thy foes.

My God, Man cannot praise thy name:
Thou art all brightnesse, perfect puritie;
   The sunne holds down his head for shame,
Dead with eclipses, when we speak of thee:
        How shall infection
        Presume on thy perfection?

As dirtie hands foul all they touch,
And those things most, which are most pure and fine:
   So our clay hearts, ev'n when we crouch
To sing thy praises, make them less divine.
        Yet either this,
        Or none, thy portion is.

Man cannot serve thee; let him go,
And serve the swine: there, there is his delight:
   He doth not like this vertue, no;
Give him his dirt to wallow in all night:
        These Preachers make
        His head to shoot and ake.

Oh foolish man! where are thine eyes?
How hast thou lost them in a croud of cares?
   Thou pull'st the rug, and wilt not rise,
No, not to purchase the whole pack of starres:
        There let them shine,
        Thou must go sleep, or dine.

The bird that sees a daintie bowre
Made in the tree, where she was wont to sit,
   Wonders and sings, but not his power
Who made the arbour: this exceeds her wit.
         But Man doth know
           The spring, whence all things flow:

And yet, as though he knew it not,
His knowledge winks, and lets his humours reigne,
   They make his life a constant blot,
And all the bloud of God to run in vain.
         Ah wretch! what verse
           Can thy strange wayes rehearse?

Indeed at first Man was a treasure,
A box of jewels, shop of rarities,
   A ring, whose posie was, *My pleasure*:
He was a garden in a Paradise:
         Glorie and grace
           Did crown his heart and face.

But sinne hath fool'd him. Now he is
A lump of flesh, without a foot or wing
   To raise him to a glimpse of blisse:
A sick toss'd vessel, dashing on each thing;
         Nay, his own shelf:
           My God, I mean my self.

The British Church

I joy, deare Mother, when I view
Thy perfect lineaments and hue
    Both sweet and bright.
Beautie in thee takes up her place,
And dates her letters from thy face,
    When she doth write.

A fine aspect in fit aray,
Neither too mean, nor yet too gay,
    Shows who is best.
Outlandish looks may not compare:
For all they either painted are,
    Or else undrest.

She on the hills, which wantonly
Allureth all in hope to be
    By her preferr'd,
Hath kiss'd so long her painted shrines,
That ev'n her face by kissing shines,
    For her reward.

She in the valley is so shie
Of dressing, that her hair doth lie
    About her eares:
While she avoids her neighbours pride,
She wholly goes on th' other side,
    And nothing wears.

But, dearest Mother, what those misse,
The mean, thy praise and glorie is,
    And long may be.

Blessed be God, whose love it was
To double-moat thee with his grace,
                    And none but thee.

The Quip

The merrie world did on a day
With his train-bands and mates agree
To meet together, where I lay,
And all in sport to geere at me.

First, Beautie crept into a rose,
Which when I pluckt not, Sir, said she,
Tell me, I pray, Whose hands are those?
But thou shalt answer, Lord, for me.

Then Money came, and chinking still,
What tune is this, poore man? said he:
I heard in Musick you had skill.
But thou shalt answer, Lord, for me.

Then came brave Glorie puffing by
In silks that whistled, who but he?
He scarce allow'd me half an eie.
But thou shalt answer, Lord, for me.

Then came quick Wit and Conversation,
And he would needs a comfort be,
And, to be short, make an Oration.
But thou shalt answer, Lord, for me.

Yet when the houre of thy designe
To answer these fine things shall come;
Speak not at large; say, I am thine:
And then they have their answer home.

Providence

O sacred Providence, who from end to end
Strongly and sweetly movest, shall I write,
And not of thee, through whom my fingers bend
To hold my quill? shall they not do thee right?

Of all the creatures both in sea and land
Onely to Man thou hast made known thy wayes,
And put the penne alone into his hand,
And made him Secretarie of thy praise.

Beasts fain would sing; birds dittie to their notes;
Trees would be tuning on their native lute
To thy renown: but all their hands and throats
Are brought to Man, while they are lame and mute.

Man is the worlds high Priest: he doth present
The sacrifice for all; while they below
Unto the service mutter an assent,
Such as springs use that fall, and windes that blow.

He that to praise and laud thee doth refrain,
Doth not refrain unto himself alone,
But robs a thousand who would praise thee fain,
And doth commit a world of sinne in one.

The beasts say, Eat me: but, if beasts must teach,
The tongue is yours to eat, but mine to praise.
The trees say, Pull me: but the hand you stretch,
Is mine to write, as it is yours to raise.

Wherefore, most sacred Spirit, I here present
For me and all my fellows praise to thee:
And just it is that I should pay the rent,
Because the benefit accrues to me.

We all acknowledge both thy power and love
To be exact, transcendent, and divine;
Who dost so strongly and so sweetly move,
While all things have their will, yet none but thine.

For either thy command or thy permission
Lay hands on all: they are thy right and left.
The first puts on with speed and expedition;
The other curbs sinnes stealing pace and theft.

Nothing escapes them both; all must appeare,
And be dispos'd, and dress'd, and tun'd by thee,
Who sweetly temper'st all. If we could heare
Thy skill and art, what musick would it be!

Thou art in small things great, not small in any:
Thy even praise can neither rise, nor fall.
Thou art in all things one, in each thing many:
For thou art infinite in one and all.

Tempests are calm to thee; they know thy hand,
And hold it fast, as children do their fathers,
Which crie and follow. Thou hast made poore sand
Check the proud sea, ev'n when it swells and gathers.

Thy cupboard serves the world: the meat is set,
Where all may reach: no beast but knows his feed.
Birds teach us hawking; fishes have their net:
The great prey on the lesse, they on some weed.

Nothing ingendred doth prevent his meat:
Flies have their table spread, ere they appeare.
Some creatures have in winter what to eat;
Others do sleep, and envie not their cheer.

How finely dost thou times and seasons spin,
And make a twist checker'd with night and day!
Which as it lengthens windes, and windes us in,
As bouls go on, but turning all the way.

Each creature hath a wisdome for his good.
The pigeons feed their tender off-spring, crying,
When they are callow; but withdraw their food
When they are fledge, that need may teach them flying.

Bees work for man; and yet they never bruise
Their masters flower, but leave it, having done,
As fair as ever, and as fit to use;
So both the flower doth stay, and hony run.

Sheep eat the grasse, and dung the ground for more:
Trees after bearing drop their leaves for soil:
Springs vent their streams, and by expense get store:
Clouds cool by heat, and baths by cooling boil.

Who hath the vertue to expresse the rare
And curious vertues both of herbs and stones?
Is there an herb for that? O that thy care
Would show a root, that gives expressions!

And if an herb hath power, what have the starres?
A rose, besides his beautie, is a cure.
Doubtlesse our plagues and plentie, peace and warres
Are there much surer then our art is sure.

Thou hast hid metals: man may take them thence;
But at his perill: when he digs the place,
He makes a grave; as if the thing had sense,
And threatned man, that he should fill the space.

Ev'n poysons praise thee. Should a thing be lost?
Should creatures want for want of heed their due?
Since where are poysons, antidotes are most:
The help stands close, and keeps the fear in view.

The sea, which seems to stop the traveller,
Is by a ship the speedier passage made.
The windes, who think they rule the mariner,
Are rul'd by him, and taught to serve his trade.

And as thy house is full, so I adore
Thy curious art in marshalling thy goods.
The hills with health abound; the vales with store;
The South with marble; North with furres & woods.

Hard things are glorious: easie things good cheap.
The common all men have; that which is rare
Men therefore seek to have, and care to keep.
The healthy frosts with summer-fruits compare.

Light without winde is glasse: warm without weight
Is wooll and furre: cool without closenesse, shade:
Speed without pains, a horse: tall without height,
A servile hawk: low without losse, a spade.

All countreys have enough to serve their need:
If they seek fine things, thou dost make them run
For their offence; and then dost turn their speed
To be commerce and trade from sunne to sunne.

Nothing wears clothes, but Man; nothing doth need
But he to wear them. Nothing useth fire,
But Man alone, to show his heav'nly breed:
And onely he hath fuell in desire.

When th' earth was dry, thou mad'st a sea of wet:
When that lay gather'd, thou didst broach the mountains:
When yet some places could no moisture get,
The windes grew gard'ners, and the clouds good fountains.

Rain, do not hurt my flowers; but gently spend
Your hony drops: presse not to smell them here:
When they are ripe, their odour will ascend,
And at your lodging with their thanks appeare.

How harsh are thorns to pears! and yet they make
A better hedge, and need lesse reparation.
How smooth are silks compared with a stake,
Or with a stone! yet make no good foundation.

Sometimes thou dost divide thy gifts to man,
Sometimes unite. The Indian nut alone
Is clothing, meat and trencher, drink and can,
Boat, cable, sail and needle, all in one.

Most herbs that grow in brooks, are hot and dry.
Cold fruits warm kernells help against the winde.
The lemmons juice and rinde cure mutually.
The whey of milk doth loose, the milk doth binde.

Thy creatures leap not, but expresse a feast,
Where all the guests sit close, and nothing wants.
Frogs marry fish and flesh; bats, bird and beast;
Sponges, non-sense and sense; mines, th' earth & plants.

To show thou art not bound, as if thy lot
Were worse then ours, sometimes thou shiftest hands.
Most things move th' under-jaw; the Crocodile not.
Most things sleep lying; th' Elephant leans or stands.

But who hath praise enough? nay, who hath any?
None can expresse thy works, but he that knows them:
And none can know thy works, which are so many,
And so complete, but onely he that owes them.

All things that are, though they have sev'rall wayes,
Yet in their being joyn with one advise
To honour thee: and so I give thee praise
In all my other hymnes, but in this twice.

Each thing that is, although in use and name
It go for one, hath many wayes in store
To honour thee; and so each hymne thy fame
Extolleth many wayes, yet this one more.

Hope

I gave to Hope a watch of mine: but he
                An anchor gave to me.
Then an old prayer-book I did present:
                And he an optick sent.
With that I gave a viall full of tears:
                But he a few green eares.
Ah Loyterer! I'le no more, no more I'le bring:
                I did expect a ring.

Sinnes Round

Sorrie I am, my God, sorrie I am,
That my offences course it in a ring.
My thoughts are working like a busie flame,
Untill their cockatrice they hatch and bring:
And when they once have perfected their draughts,
My words take fire from my inflamed thoughts.

My words take fire from my inflamed thoughts,
Which spit it forth like the Sicilian Hill.
They vent the wares, and passe them with their faults,
And by their breathing ventilate the ill.
But words suffice not, where are lewd intentions:
My hands do joyn to finish the inventions.

My hands do joyn to finish the inventions:
And so my sinnes ascend three stories high,
As Babel grew, before there were dissensions.
Yet ill deeds loyter not: for they supplie
New thoughts of sinning: wherefore, to my shame,
Sorrie I am, my God, sorrie I am.

Peace

Sweet Peace, where dost thou dwell? I humbly crave,
            Let me once know.
    I sought thee in a secret cave,
      And ask'd, if Peace were there.
A hollow winde did seem to answer, No:
            Go seek elsewhere.

I did; and going did a rainbow note:
            Surely, thought I,
    This is the lace of Peaces coat:
      I will search out the matter.
But while I lookt, the clouds immediately
            Did break and scatter.

Then went I to a garden, and did spy
            A gallant flower,
    The Crown Imperiall: Sure, said I,
      Peace at the root must dwell.
But when I digg'd, I saw a worm devoure
            What show'd so well.

At length I met a rev'rend good old man,
            Whom when for Peace
    I did demand, he thus began:
      There was a Prince of old
At Salem dwelt, who liv'd with good increase
            Of flock and fold.

He sweetly liv'd; yet sweetnesse did not save
             His life from foes.
    But after death out of his grave
        There sprang twelve stalks of wheat:
Which many wondring at, got some of those
           To plant and set.

It prosper'd strangely, and did soon disperse
           Through all the earth:
    For they that taste it do rehearse,
       That vertue lies therein,
A secret vertue bringing peace and mirth
          By flight of sinne.

Take of this grain, which in my garden grows,
          And grows for you;
    Make bread of it: and that repose
      And peace, which ev'ry where
With so much earnestnesse you do pursue,
        Is onely there.

Mans Medley

Heark, how the birds do sing,
And woods do ring.
All creatures have their joy: and man hath his.
Yet if we rightly measure,
Mans joy and pleasure
Rather hereafter, then in present, is.

To this life things of sense
Make their pretence:
In th' other Angels have a right by birth:
Man ties them both alone,
And makes them one,
With th' one hand touching heav'n, with th' other earth.

In soul he mounts and flies,
In flesh he dies.
He wears a stuffe whose thread is course and round,
But trimm'd with curious lace,
And should take place
After the trimming, not the stuffe and ground.

Not that he may not here
Taste of the cheer,
But as birds drink, and straight lift up their head,
So he must sip and think
Of better drink
He may attain to, after he is dead.

But as his joyes are double;
So is his trouble.
He hath two winters, other things but one:

Both frosts and thoughts do nip,
                And bite his lip;
And he of all things fears two deaths alone.

                Yet ev'n the greatest griefs
                May be reliefs,
Could he but take them right, and in their wayes.
                Happie is he, whose heart
                Hath found the art
To turn his double pains to double praise.

The Storm

If as the windes and waters here below
                Do flie and flow,
My sighs and tears as busie were above;
                Sure they would move
And much affect thee, as tempestuous times
Amaze poore mortals, and object their crimes.

Starres have their storms, ev'n in a high degree,
                As well as we.
A throbbing conscience spurred by remorse
                Hath a strange force:
It quits the earth, and mounting more and more
Dares to assault thee, and besiege thy doore.

There it stands knocking, to thy musicks wrong,
                And drowns the song.
Glorie and honour are set by, till it
                An answer get.
Poets have wrong'd poore storms: such dayes are best,
They purge the aire without, within the breast.

Artillerie

As I one ev'ning sat before my cell,
Me thoughts a starre did shoot into my lap.
I rose, and shook my clothes, as knowing well,
That from small fires comes oft no small mishap.
    When suddenly I heard one say,
    Do as thou usest, disobey,
    Expell good motions from thy breast,
Which have the face of fire, but end in rest.

I, who had heard of musick in the spheres,
But not of speech in starres, began to muse:
But turning to my God, whose ministers
The starres and all things are; If I refuse,
    Dread Lord, said I, so oft my good;
    Then I refuse not ev'n with bloud
    To wash away my stubborn thought:
For I will do or suffer what I ought.

But I have also starres and shooters too,
Born where thy servants both artilleries use.
My tears and prayers night and day do wooe,
And work up to thee; yet thou dost refuse.
    Not but I am (I must say still)
    Much more oblig'd to do thy will,
    Then thou to grant mine: but because
Thy promise now hath ev'n set thee thy laws.

Then we are shooters both, and thou dost deigne
To enter combate with us, and contest
With thine own clay. But I would parley fain:
Shunne not my arrows, and behold my breast.

Yet if thou shunnest, I am thine:
I must be so, if I am mine.
There is no articling with thee:
I am but finite, yet thine infinitely.

The Pilgrimage

I travell'd on, seeing the hill, where lay
                    My expectation.
            A long it was and weary way.
            The gloomy cave of Desperation
I left on th' one, and on the other side
                    The rock of Pride.

And so I came to Fancies medow strow'd
                    With many a flower:
            Fain would I here have made abode,
            But I was quicken'd by my houre.
So to Cares cops I came, and there got through
                    With much ado.

That led me to the wilde of Passion, which
                    Some call the wold;
            A wasted place, but sometimes rich.
            Here I was robb'd of all my gold,
Save one good Angell, which a friend had ti'd
                    Close to my side.

At length I got unto the gladsome hill,
                    Where lay my hope,
            Where lay my heart; and climbing still,
            When I had gain'd the brow and top,
A lake of brackish waters on the ground
                    Was all I found.

With that abash'd and struck with many a sting
                    Of swarming fears,
            I fell, and cry'd, Alas my King!

Can both the way and end be tears?
Yet taking heart I rose, and then perceiv'd
                    I was deceiv'd:

My hill was further: so I flung away,
                    Yet heard a crie
            Just as I went, *None goes that way*
            And lives : If that be all, said I,
After so foul a journey death is fair,
                    And but a chair.

The Discharge

Busie enquiring heart, what wouldst thou know?
                Why dost thou prie,
And turn, and leer, and with a licorous eye
                Look high and low;
           And in thy lookings stretch and grow?

Hast thou not made thy counts, and summ'd up all?
                Did not thy heart
Give up the whole, and with the whole depart?
                Let what will fall:
           That which is past who can recall?

Thy life is Gods, thy time to come is gone,
                And is his right.
He is thy night at noon: he is at night
                Thy noon alone.
           The crop is his, for he hath sown.

And well it was for thee, when this befell,
                That God did make
Thy businesse his, and in thy life partake:
                For thou canst tell,
           If it be his once, all is well.

Onely the present is thy part and fee.
                And happy thou,
If, though thou didst not beat thy future brow,
                Thou couldst well see
           What present things requir'd of thee.

They ask enough; why shouldst thou further go?
                Raise not the mudde
Of future depths, but drink the cleare and good.
                Dig not for wo
       In times to come; for it will grow.

Man and the present fit: if he provide,
                He breaks the square.
This houre is mine: if for the next I care,
                I grow too wide,
       And do encroach upon deaths side.

For death each houre environs and surrounds.
                He that would know
And care for future chances, cannot go
                Unto those grounds,
       But through a Church-yard which them bounds.

Things present shrink and die: but they that spend
                Their thoughts and sense
On future grief, do not remove it thence,
                But it extend,
       And draw the bottome out an end.

God chains the dog till night: wilt loose the chain,
                And wake thy sorrow?
Wilt thou forestall it, and now grieve to morrow,
                And then again
       Grieve over freshly all thy pain?

Either grief will not come: or if it must,
                Do not forecast.
And while it cometh, it is almost past.
                Always distrust:
       My God hath promis'd; he is just.

The Collar

I struck the board, and cry'd, No more.
                        I will abroad.
      What? shall I ever sigh and pine?
My lines and life are free; free as the rode,
        Loose as the winde, as large as store.
                 Shall I be still in suit?
      Have I no harvest but a thorn
      To let me bloud, and not restore
      What I have lost with cordiall fruit?
                    Sure there was wine
Before my sighs did drie it: there was corn
          Before my tears did drown it.
      Is the yeare onely lost to me?
            Have I no bayes to crown it?
No flowers, no garlands gay? all blasted?
                All wasted?
      Not so, my heart: but there is fruit,
          And thou hast hands.
Recover all thy sigh-blown age
On double pleasures: leave thy cold dispute
Of what is fit, and not. Forsake thy cage,
         Thy rope of sands,
Which pettie thoughts have made, and made to thee
      Good cable, to enforce and draw,
           And be thy law,
While thou didst wink and wouldst not see.
           Away; take heed:
           I will abroad.
Call in thy deaths head there: tie up thy fears.
         He that forbears
        To suit and serve his need,

          Deserves his load.
But as I rav'd and grew more fierce and wilde
          At every word,
Me thoughts I heard one calling, *Child!*
          And I reply'd, *My Lord*.

Clasping of Hands

Lord, thou art mine, and I am thine,
If mine I am: and thine much more,
Then I or ought, or can be mine.
Yet to be thine, doth me restore;
So that again I now am mine,
And with advantage mine the more,
Since this being mine, brings with it thine,
And thou with me dost thee restore.
    If I without thee would be mine,
    I neither should be mine nor thine.

Lord, I am thine, and thou art mine:
So mine thou art, that something more
I may presume thee mine, then thine.
For thou didst suffer to restore
Not thee, but me, and to be mine,
And with advantage mine the more,
Since thou in death wast none of thine,
Yet then as mine didst me restore.
    O be mine still! still make me thine!
    Or rather make no Thine and Mine!

Praise

Lord, I will mean and speak thy praise,
                    Thy praise alone.
My busie heart shall spin it all my dayes:
        And when it stops for want of store,
Then will I wring it with a sigh or grone,
                    That thou mayst yet have more.

When thou dost favour any action,
                    It runnes, it flies:
All things concurre to give it a perfection.
        That which had but two legs before,
When thou dost blesse, hath twelve: one wheel doth rise
                    To twentie then, or more.

But when thou dost on businesse blow,
                    It hangs, it clogs:
Not all the teams of Albion in a row
        Can hale or draw it out of doore.
Legs are but stumps, and Pharaohs wheels but logs,
                    And struggling hinders more.

Thousands of things do thee employ
                    In ruling all
This spacious globe: Angels must have their joy,
        Devils their rod, the sea his shore,
The windes their stint: and yet when I did call,
                    Thou heardst my call, and more.

I have not lost one single tear:
                But when mine eyes
Did weep to heav'n, they found a bottle there
    (As we have boxes for the poore)
Readie to take them in; yet of a size
          That would contain much more.

But after thou hadst slipt a drop
               From thy right eye,
(Which there did hang like streamers neare the top
    Of some fair church, to show the sore
And bloudie battell which thou once didst trie)
         The glasse was full and more.

Wherefore I sing. Yet since my heart,
              Though press'd, runnes thin;
O that I might some other hearts convert,
    And so take up at use good store:
That to thy chest there might be coming in
         Both all my praise, and more!

The Flower

How fresh, O Lord, how sweet and clean
Are thy returns! ev'n as the flowers in spring;
To which, besides their own demean,
The late-past frosts tributes of pleasure bring.
Grief melts away
Like snow in May,
As if there were no such cold thing.

Who would have thought my shrivel'd heart
Could have recover'd greennesse? It was gone
Quite under ground; as flowers depart
To see their mother-root, when they have blown;
Where they together
All the hard weather,
Dead to the world, keep house unknown.

These are thy wonders, Lord of power,
Killing and quickning, bringing down to hell
And up to heaven in an houre;
Making a chiming of a passing-bell.
We say amisse,
This or that is:
Thy word is all, if we could spell.

O that I once past changing were,
Fast in thy Paradise, where no flower can wither!
Many a spring I shoot up fair,
Offring at heav'n, growing and groning thither:
Nor doth my flower
Want a spring-showre,
My sinnes and I joining together.

But while I grow in a straight line,
Still upwards bent, as if heav'n were mine own,
   Thy anger comes, and I decline:
What frost to that? what pole is not the zone,
        Where all things burn,
        When thou dost turn,
  And the least frown of thine is shown?

   And now in age I bud again,
After so many deaths I live and write;
   I once more smell the dew and rain,
And relish versing: O my onely light,
        It cannot be
        That I am he
On whom thy tempests fell all night.

   These are thy wonders, Lord of love,
To make us see we are but flowers that glide:
   Which when we once can finde and prove,
Thou hast a garden for us, where to bide.
        Who would be more,
        Swelling through store,
Forfeit their Paradise by their pride.

Aaron

Holinesse on the head,
Light and perfections on the breast,
Harmonious bells below, raising the dead
To leade them unto life and rest:
Thus are true Aarons drest.

Profanenesse in my head,
Defects and darknesse in my breast,
A noise of passions ringing me for dead
Unto a place where is no rest:
Poore priest thus am I drest.

Onely another head
I have, another heart and breast,
Another musick, making live not dead,
Without whom I could have no rest:
In him I am well drest.

Christ is my onely head,
My alone onely heart and breast,
My onely musick, striking me ev'n dead;
That to the old man I may rest,
And be in him new drest.

So holy in my head,
Perfect and light in my deare breast,
My doctrine tun'd by Christ, (who is not dead,
But lives in me while I do rest)
Come people; Aaron's drest.

The Odour

How sweetly doth *My Master* sound! *My Master!*
　　　　As Amber-greese leaves a rich sent
　　　　　　　Unto the taster:
　　　　So do these words a sweet content,
An orientall fragrancie, *My Master*.

With these all day I do perfume my minde,
　　　　My minde ev'n thrust into them both:
　　　　　　　That I might finde
　　　　What cordials make this curious broth,
This broth of smells, that feeds and fats my minde.

My Master, shall I speak? O that to thee
　　　　My servant were a little so,
　　　　　　　As flesh may be;
　　　　That these two words might creep & grow
To some degree of spicinesse to thee!

Then should the Pomander, which was before
　　　　A sparkling sweet, mend by reflection,
　　　　　　　And tell me more:
　　　　For pardon of my imperfection
Would warm and work it sweeter then before.

For when *My Master*, which alone is sweet,
　　　　And ev'n in my unworthinesse pleasing,
　　　　　　　Shall call and meet,
　　　　My servant, as thee not displeasing,
That call is but the breathing of the sweet.

This breathing would with gains by sweetning me
      (As sweet things traffick when they meet)
           Return to thee.
   And so this new commerce and sweet
Should all my life employ and busie me.

The Elixir

Teach me, my God and King,
   In all things thee to see,
And what I do in any thing,
   To do it as for thee:

Not rudely, as a beast,
   To runne into an action;
But still to make thee prepossest,
   And give it his perfection.

A man that looks on glasse,
   On it may stay his eye;
Or if he pleaseth, through it passe,
   And then the heav'n espie.

All may of thee partake:
   Nothing can be so mean,
Which with his tincture (for thy sake)
   Will not grow bright and clean.

A servant with this clause
   Makes drudgerie divine:
Who sweeps a room, as for thy laws,
   Makes that and th' action fine.

This is the famous stone
   That turneth all to gold:
For that which God doth touch and own
   Cannot for lesse be told.

Dooms-Day

Come away,
Make no delay.
Summon all the dust to rise,
Till it stirre, and rubbe the eyes;
While this member jogs the other,
Each one whispring, *Live you brother?*

Come away,
Make this the day.
Dust, alas, no musick feels,
But thy trumpet: then it kneels,
As peculiar notes and strains
Cure Tarantulas raging pains.

Come away,
O make no stay!
Let the graves make their confession,
Lest at length they plead possession:
Fleshes stubbornnesse may have
Read that lesson to the grave.

Come away,
Thy flock doth stray.
Some to windes their bodie lend,
And in them may drown a friend:
Some in noisome vapours grow
To a plague and publick wo.

Come away,
Help our decay.
Man is out of order hurl'd,
Parcel'd out to all the world.
Lord, thy broken consort raise,
And the musick shall be praise.

Heaven

O who will show me those delights on high?
        Echo.   I.
Thou Echo, thou art mortall, all men know.
        Echo.   No.
Wert thou not born among the trees and leaves?
        Echo.   Leaves.
And are there any leaves, that still abide?
        Echo.   Bide.
What leaves are they? impart the matter wholly.
        Echo.   Holy.
Are holy leaves the Echo then of blisse?
        Echo.   Yes.
Then tell me, what is that supreme delight?
        Echo.   Light.
Light to the minde: what shall the will enjoy?
        Echo.   Joy.
But are there cares and businesse with the pleasure?
        Echo.   Leisure.
Light, joy, and leisure; but shall they persever?
        Echo.   Ever.

Love

Love bade me welcome: yet my soul drew back,
              Guiltie of dust and sinne.
But quick-ey'd Love, observing me grow slack
              From my first entrance in,
Drew nearer to me, sweetly questioning,
              If I lack'd any thing.

A guest, I answer'd, worthy to be here:
              Love said, You shall be he.
I the unkinde, ungratefull? Ah my deare,
              I cannot look on thee.
Love took my hand, and smiling did reply,
              Who made the eyes but I?

Truth Lord, but I have marr'd them: let my shame
              Go where it doth deserve.
And know you not, sayes Love, who bore the blame?
              My deare, then I will serve.
You must sit down, sayes Love, and taste my meat:
              So I did sit and eat.

The Church Militant

Almightie Lord, who from thy glorious throne
Seest and rulest all things ev'n as one:
The smallest ant or atome knows thy power,
Known also to each minute of an houre:
Much more do Common-weals acknowledge thee,
And wrap their policies in thy decree,
Complying with thy counsels, doing nought
Which doth not meet with an eternall thought.
But above all, thy Church and Spouse doth prove
Not the decrees of power, but bands of love.
Early didst thou arise to plant this vine,
Which might the more indeare it to be thine.
Spices come from the East; so did thy Spouse,
Trimme as the light, sweet as the laden boughs
Of *Noahs* shadie vine, chaste as the dove;
Prepar'd and fitted to receive thy love.
The course was westward, that the sunne might light
As well our understanding as our sight.
Where th' Ark did rest, there *Abraham* began
To bring the other Ark from *Canaan.*
Moses pursu'd this: but King *Solomon*
Finish'd and fixt the old religion.
When it grew loose, the Jews did hope in vain
By nailing Christ to fasten it again.
But to the Gentiles he bore crosse and all,
Rending with earthquakes the partition-wall:
Onely whereas the Ark in glorie shone,
Now with the crosse, as with a staffe, alone,
Religion, like a pilgrime, westward bent,
Knocking at all doores, ever as she went.
Yet as the sunne, though forward be his flight,

Listens behinde him, and allows some light,
Till all depart: so went the Church her way,
Letting, while one foot stept, the other stay
Among the eastern nations for a time,
Till both removed to the western clime.
To *Egypt* first she came, where they did prove
Wonders of anger once, but now of love.
The ten Commandments there did flourish more
Then the ten bitter plagues had done before.
Holy *Macarius* and great *Anthonie*
Made *Pharaoh Moses*, changing th' historie.
Goshen was darknesse, *Egypt* full of lights,
Nilus for monsters brought forth Israelites.
Such power hath mightie Baptisme to produce
For things misshapen, things of highest use.
How deare to me, O God, thy counsels are !
              Who may with thee compare ?
Religion thence fled into *Greece*, where arts
Gave her the highest place in all mens hearts.
Learning was pos'd, Philosophie was set,
Sophisters taken in a fishers net.
Plato and *Aristotle* were at a losse,
And wheel'd about again to spell *Christ-Crosse*.
Prayers chas'd syllogismes into their den,
And *Ergo* was transform'd into *Amen*.
Though *Greece* took horse as soon as *Egypt* did,
And *Rome* as both; yet *Egypt* faster rid,
And spent her period and prefixed time
Before the other. *Greece* being past her prime,
Religion went to *Rome*, subduing those,
Who, that they might subdue, made all their foes.
The Warrier his deere skarres no more resounds,
But seems to yeeld Christ hath the greater wounds,
Wounds willingly endur'd to work his blisse,

Who by an ambush lost his Paradise.
The great heart stoops, and taketh from the dust
A sad repentance, not the spoils of lust:
Quitting his spear, lest it should pierce again
Him in his members, who for him was slain.
The Shepherds hook grew to a scepter here,
Giving new names and numbers to the yeare.
But th' Empire dwelt in *Greece*, to comfort them
Who were cut short in *Alexanders* stemme.
In both of these Prowesse and Arts did tame
And tune mens hearts against the Gospel came:
Which using, and not fearing skill in th' one,
Or strength in th' other, did erect her throne.
Many a rent and struggling th' Empire knew,
(As dying things are wont) untill it flew
At length to *Germanie*, still westward bending,
And there the Churches festivall attending:
That as before Empire and Arts made way,
(For no lesse Harbingers would serve then they)
So they might still, and point us out the place
Where first the Church should raise her down-cast
     face.
Strength levels grounds, Art makes a garden there;
Then showres Religion, and makes all to bear.
Spain in the Empire shar'd with *Germanie*,
But *England* in the higher victorie:
Giving the Church a crown to keep her state,
And not go lesse then she had done of late.
Constantines British line meant this of old,
And did this mysterie wrap up and fold
Within a sheet of paper, which was rent
From times great Chronicle, and hither sent.
Thus both the Church and Sunne together ran
Unto the farthest old meridian.

How deare to me, O God, thy counsels are!
                    Who may with thee compare?
Much about one and the same time and place,
Both where and when the Church began her race,
Sinne did set out of Eastern *Babylon*,
And travell'd westward also: journeying on
He chid the Church away, where e're he came,
Breaking her peace, and tainting her good name.
At first he got to *Egypt*, and did sow
Gardens of gods, which ev'ry yeare did grow
Fresh and fine dcities. They were at great cost,
Who for a god clearely a sallet lost.
Ah, what a thing is man devoid of grace,
Adoring garlick with an humble face,
Begging his food of that which he may eat,
Starving the while he worshippeth his meat!
Who makes a root his god, how low is he,
If God and man be sever'd infinitely!
What wretchednesse can give him any room,
Whose house is foul, while he adores his broom?
None will beleeve this now, though money be
In us the same transplanted foolerie.
Thus Sinne in *Egypt* sneaked for a while;
His highest was an ox or crocodile,
And such poore game. Thence he to *Greece* doth passe,
And being craftier much then Goodnesse was,
He left behinde him garrisons of sinnes
To make good that which ev'ry day he winnes.
Here Sinne took heart, and for a garden-bed
Rich shrines and oracles he purchased:
He grew a gallant, and would needs foretell
As well what should befall, as what befell.
Nay, he became a poet, and would serve
His pills of sublimate in that conserve.

The world came in with hands and purses full
To this great lotterie, and all would pull.
But all was glorious cheating, brave deceit,
Where some poore truths were shuffled for a bait
To credit him, and to discredit those
Who after him should braver truths disclose.
From *Greece* he went to *Rome :* and as before
He was a God, now he's an Emperour.
Nero and others lodg'd him bravely. there,
Put him in trust to rule the Romans sphere.
Glorie was his chief instrument of old:
Pleasure succeeded straight, when that grew cold.
Which soon was blown to such a mightie flame,
That though our Saviour did destroy the game,
Disparking oracles, and all their treasure,
Setting affliction to encounter pleasure;
Yet did a rogue with hope of carnall joy
Cheat the most subtill nations. Who so coy,
So trimme, as *Greece* and *Egypt ?* yet their hearts
Are given over, for their curious arts,
To such Mahometan stupidities,
As the old heathen would deem prodigies.
How deare to me, O God, thy counsels are !
        Who may with thee compare ?
Onely the West and *Rome* do keep them free
From this contagious infidelitie.
And this is all the Rock, whereof they boast,
As *Rome* will one day finde unto her cost.
Sinne being not able to extirpate quite
The Churches here, bravely resolv'd one night
To be a Church-man too, and wear a Mitre:
The old debauched ruffian would turn writer.
I saw him in his studie, where he sate
Busie in controversies sprung of late.

A gown and pen became him wondrous well:
His grave aspect had more of heav'n then hell:
Onely there was a handsome picture by,
To which he lent a corner of his eye.
As Sinne in *Greece* a Prophet was before,
And in old *Rome* a mightie Emperour;
So now being Priest he plainly did professe
To make a jest of Christs three offices:
The rather since his scatter'd jugglings were
United now in one both time and sphere.
From *Egypt* he took pettie deities,
From *Greece* oracular infallibilities,
And from old *Rome* the libertie of pleasure
By free dispensings of the Churches treasure.
Then in memoriall of his ancient throne
He did surname his palace, *Babylon*.
Yet that he might the better gain all nations,
And make that name good by their transmigrations,
From all these places, but at divers times,
He took fine vizards to conceal his crimes:
From *Egypt* Anchorisme and retirednesse,
Learning from *Greece*, from old *Rome* statelinesse:
And blending these he carri'd all mens eyes,
While Truth sat by, counting his victories:
Whereby he grew apace and scorn'd to use
Such force as once did captivate the Jews;
But did bewitch, and finely work each nation
Into a voluntarie transmigration.
All poste to *Rome :* Princes submit their necks
Either t' his publick foot or private tricks.
It did not fit his gravitie to stirre,
Nor his long journey, nor his gout and furre.
Therefore he sent out able ministers,
Statesmen within, without doores cloisterers:

Who without spear, or sword, or other drumme
Then what was in their tongue, did overcome;
And having conquer'd, did so strangely rule,
That the whole world did seem but the Popes mule.

from A Priest to the Temple

THE PARSON IN HIS HOUSE

The Parson is very exact in the governing of his house, making it a copy and modell for his Parish. He knows the temper, and pulse of every person in his house, and accordingly either meets with their vices, or advanceth their vertues. His wife is either religious, or night and day he is winning her to it. In stead of the qualities of the world, he requires onely three of her; first, a trayning up of her children and mayds in the fear of God, with prayers, and catechizing, and all religious duties. Secondly, a curing, and healing of all wounds and sores with her owne hands; which skill either she brought with her, or he takes care she shall learn it of some religious neighbour. Thirdly, a providing for her family in such sort, as that neither they want a competent sustentation, nor her husband be brought in debt. His children he first makes Christians, and then Common-wealths-men; the one he owes to his heavenly Countrey, the other to his earthly, having no title to either, except he do good to both. Therefore having seasoned them with all Piety, not only of words in praying, and reading; but in actions, in visiting other sick children, and tending their wounds, and sending his charity by them to the poor, and somtimes giving them a little mony to do it of themselves, that they get a delight in it, and enter favour with God, who weighs even childrens actions, 1 *King*. 14. 12, 13. He afterwards turnes his care to fit all their dispositions with some calling, not sparing the eldest, but giving him the prerogative of his Fathers profession, which happily for his other children he is not able to do. Yet in binding them prentices (in case he think fit to do so) he takes care not to put them into vain trades, and unbefitting the reverence of their Fathers calling, such as are tavernes for men, and lace-making for women; because those trades, for the most part, serve but the vices and vanities of the world, which he is to deny, and not augment. However, he resolves with himself never to omit any present good deed of charity, in consideration of providing a stock for his children; but assures himselfe, that mony thus lent to God, is placed surer for his childrens advantage, then if it were given to the Chamber of *London*. Good deeds, and good breeding, are his two great stocks for his children; if God give any thing above those, and not spent in them, he blesseth God, and lays it out as he sees cause. His servants are all religious, and were it not his duty to have them so, it were his profit, for none are so well served, as by religious servants, both because they do best, and because what they do, is blessed, and prospers. After religion, he teacheth them, that three things make a compleate servant, Truth, and Diligence, and Neatnesse, or Cleanlinesse. Those that can read, are allowed times for it, and those that cannot, are taught; for all in his house are either teachers or learners, or both, so that his family is a Schoole of Religion, and they all account, that to teach the ignorant is the greatest almes. Even the wals are not idle, but something is written, or painted there, which may excite the reader to a thought of piety; especially the 101 *Psalm*, which is expressed in a fayre table, as being the rule of a family. And when they go abroad, his wife among her neighbours is the beginner of good discourses, his children among children, his servants among other servants; so that as in the house of those that are skill'd in Musick, all are Musicians; so in the house of a Preacher, all are preachers. He suffers not a ly or equivocation by any means in his house, but counts it the art, and secret of governing to preserve a directnesse, and open plainnesse in all things; so that all his house knowes, that there is no help for a fault done, but confession. He *himselfe*, or his *Wife*, takes account of Sermons, and how every one profits, comparing this yeer with the last: and besides the common prayers of the family, he straitly requires of all to pray by them-

selves before they sleep at night, and stir out in the morning,
and knows what prayers they say, and till they have learned
them, makes them kneel by him; esteeming that this private
praying is a more voluntary act in them, then when they are
called to others prayers, and that, which when they leave the
family, they carry with them. He keeps his servants between
love, and fear, according as hee findes them; but generally he
distributes it thus, To his Children he shewes more love then
terrour, to his servants more terrour then love; but an old good
servant boards a child. The furniture of his house is very plain,
but clean, whole, and sweet, as sweet as his garden can make;
for he hath no mony for such things, charity being his only
perfume, which deserves cost when he can spare it. His fare is
plain, and common, but wholsome, what hee hath, is little, but
very good; it consisteth most of mutton, beefe, and veal, if he
addes anything for a great day, or a stranger, his garden or
orchard supplyes it, or his barne, and back-side: he goes no
further for any entertainment, lest he goe into the world,
esteeming it absurd, that he should exceed, who teacheth
others temperance. But those which his home produceth, he
refuseth not, as coming cheap, and easie, and arising from the
improvement of things, which otherwise would be lost. Where-
in he admires and imitates the wonderfull providence and
thrift of the great householder of the world: for there being
two things, which as they are, are unuseful to man, the one for
smalnesse, as crums, and scattered corn, and the like; the
other for the foulnesse, as wash, and durt, and things thereinto
fallen; God hath provided Creatures for both; for the first,
Poultry; for the second, swine. These save man the labour,
and doing that which either he could not do, or was not fit for
him to do, by taking both sorts of food into them, do as it were
dresse and prepare both for man in themselves, by growing
them selves fit for his table. The Parson in his house observes
fasting dayes; and particularly, as Sunday is his day of joy, so

Friday his day of Humiliation, which he celebrates not only with abstinence of diet, but also of company, recreation, and all outward contentments; and besides, with confessions of sins, and all acts of Mortification. Now fasting dayes containe a treble obligation; first of eating lesse that day, then on other dayes; secondly, of eating no pleasing, or over-nourishing things, as the Israelites did eate sowre herbs: Thirdly, of eating no flesh, which is but the determination of the second rule by Authority to this particular. The two former obligations are much more essentiall to a true fast, then the third and last; and fasting dayes were fully performed by keeping of the two former, had not Authority interposed: so that to eat little, and that unpleasant, is the naturall rule of fasting, although it be flesh. For since fasting in Scripture language is an afflicting of our souls, if a peece of dry flesh at my table be more unpleasant to me, then some fish there, certainly to eat the flesh, and not the fish, is to keep the fasting day naturally. And it is observable, that the prohibiting of flesh came from hot Countreys, where both flesh alone, and much more with wine, is apt to nourish more then in cold regions, and where flesh may be much better spared, and with more safety then elsewhere, where both the people and the drink being cold and flegmatick, the eating of flesh is an antidote to both. For it is certaine, that a weak stomack being prepossessed with flesh, shall much better brooke and bear a draught of beer, then if it had taken before either fish, or rootes, or such things; which will discover it selfe by spitting, and rheume, or flegme. To conclude, the Parson, if he be in full health, keeps the three obligations, eating fish, or roots, and that for quantity little, for quality unpleasant. If his body be weak and obstructed, as most Students are, he cannot keep the last obligation, nor suffer others in his house that are so, to keep it; but only the two former, which also in diseases of exinanition (as consumptions) must be broken: For meat was made for man, not man for meat. To all this may be added, not for emboldening the unruly, but for the comfort of the weak, that not onely sicknesse breaks these obligations of fasting, but sicklinesse also. For it is as unnatural to do any thing, that leads me to a sicknesse, to which I am inclined, as not to get out of that sicknesse, when I am in it, by any diet. One thing is evident, that an English body, and a Students body, are two great obstructed vessels, and there is nothing that is food, and not phisick, which doth lesse obstruct, then flesh moderately taken; as being immoderately taken, it is exceeding obstructive. And obstructions are the cause of most diseases.

from, Walton's Life of Herbert
in *The Temple*

TO HIS MOTHER, IN HER SICKNESS

Madam,

At my last parting from you, I was the better content because I was in hope I should my self carry all sickness out of your family: but since I know I did not, and that your share continues, or rather increaseth, I wish earnestly that I were again with you: and, would quickly make good my wish but that my employment does fix me here, it being now but a month to our *Commencement*: wherein, my absence by how much it naturally augmenteth suspicion, by so much shall it make my prayers the more constant and the more earnest for you to the God of all Consolation. – In the mean time, I beseech you to be chearful, and comfort your self in the God of all Comfort, who is not willing to behold any sorrow but for sin. – What hath Affliction grievous in it more then for a moment? or why should our afflictions here, have so much power or boldness as to oppose the hope of our Joyes hereafter! – *Madam!* As the Earth is but a point in respect of the heavens, so are earthly Troubles compar'd to heavenly Joyes; therefore, if either Age or Sickness lead you to those Joyes? consider what advantage you have over *Youth* and *Health*, who are now so near those true Comforts. – Your last Letter gave me Earthly preferment, and kept Heavenly for your self: but, wou'd you divide and choose too? our Colledge Customs allow not that, and I shou'd account my self most happy if I might change with you; for, I have alwaies observ'd the thred of Life to be like other threds or skenes of silk, full of snarles and incumbrances: Happy is he, whose bottom is wound up and laid ready for work in the New *Jerusalem*. – For my self, *dear Mother*, I alwaies fear'd sickness more then death, because sickness hath made me unable to perform those Offices for which I came into the world, and must yet be kept in it; but you are freed from that fear, who have already abundantly discharg'd that part, having both ordered your Family, and so brought up your Children that they have attain'd to the years of Discretion, and competent Maintenance. – So that now if they do not well the falt cannot be charg'd on you; whose Example and Care of them will justifie you both to the world and your own Conscience: insomuch, that whether you turn your thoughts on the life past, or on the Joyes that are to come, you have strong preservatives against all disquiet. – And, for temporal Afflictions! I beseech you consider all that can happen to you are either afflictions of Estate, or Body, or Mind. – For those of Estate? of what poor regard ought they to be, since if we had Riches we are commanded to give them away: so that the best use of them is, having, not to have them. – But perhaps being above the Common people, our Credit and estimation calls on us to live in a more splendid fashion? – but, Oh God! how easily is that answered, when we consider that the Blessings in the holy Scripture, are never given to the rich, but to the poor. I never find Blessed be the Rich; or, Blessed be the Noble; but, *Blessed be the Meek*, and *Blessed be the Poor*, and, *Blessed be the Mourners, for they shall be comforted*. – And yet, Oh God! most carry themselves so, as if they not only not desir'd, but, even fear'd to be blessed. – And for afflictions of the Body, *dear Madam*, remember the holy Martyrs of God, how they have been burnt by thousands, and have endur'd such other Tortures, as the very mention of them might beget amazement; but, their Fiery-tryals have had an end: and yours (which praised be God are less) are not like to continue long. – I beseech you let such thoughts as these, moderate your present fear and sorrow; and know, that if any of yours shou'd prove a *Goliah*-like trouble, yet you may say with *David*, – *That God who hath delivered me out of the paws of the Lyon and Bear, will also deliver me out of the hands of this uncircumcised* Philistin. – Lastly, for those afflictions of the Soul, consider that God intends that to be as a *sacred Temple* for himself to dwell in, and will not allow any room there for such an in-mate as Grief; or, allow that any sadness shall be his Competitor. – And above all, If any care of future things molest you? remember those admirable words of the Psalmist: *Cast thy Care on the Lord and he shall nourish thee.* (*Psal.* 55.) To which joyn that of St. *Peter, Casting all your Care on the Lord, for he careth for you.* (1 *Pet.* 5. 7.) – What an admirable thing is this, that God puts his shoulder to our burthen; and, entertains our Care for us that we may the more quietly intend his service. – To Conclude, Let me commend only one place more to you (*Philip.* 4. 4.) St. *Paul* saith there: *Rejoyce in the Lord alwaies, and again I say rejoyce.* He doubles it to take away the scruple of those that might say, What shall we rejoyce in afflictions? yes, I say again rejoyce; so that it is not left to us to rejoyce or not rejoyce: but, whatsoever befals us we must alwaies, at all times rejoyce in the Lord, who taketh care for us: and, it follows in the next verse: *Let your moderation appear to all men, the Lord is at hand: be careful for nothing.* What can be said more comfortably? trouble not your selves, God is at hand to deliver us from all, or, in all. – *Dear Madam,* pardon my boldness, and, accept the good meaning of,

> Your most obedient Son,

> GEORGE HERBERT

Trin. Col.
  May 29.
    1622.

MORE ABOUT PENGUINS AND PELICANS

Penguinews, which appears every month, contains details of all the new books issued by Penguins as they are published. From time to time it is supplemented by *Penguins in Print*, which is a complete list of all available books published by Penguins. (There are well over three thousand of these.)

A specimen copy of *Penguinews* will be sent to you free on request, and you can become a subscriber for the price of the postage. For a year's issues (including the complete lists) please send 30p if you live in the United Kingdom, or 60p if you live elsewhere. Just write to Dept EP, Penguin Books Ltd, Harmondsworth, Middlesex, enclosing a cheque or postal order, and your name will be added to the mailing list.

Note: *Penguinews* and *Penguins in Print* are not available in the U.S.A. or Canada

PENGUIN MODERN EUROPEAN POETS

This series now includes selected work by the following poets, in verse translations by, among others, W. H. Auden, Lawrence Ferlinghetti, Michael Hamburger, Ted Hughes, J. B. Leishman, Christopher Middleton and David Wevill:

Akhmatova
Amichai
Apollinaire
Bobrowski/Bienek
Celan
Ekelöf
Enzensberger
Four Greek Poets:
Cavafy/Elytis/Gatsos/Seferis
Grass
Guillevic
Haavikko/Tranströmer
Holan
Holub

Kovner/Sachs
Montale
Pavese
Pessoa
Popa
Prévert
Quasimodo
Rilke
Three Czech Poets:
Nezval/Bartušek/Hanzlík
Ungaretti
Weöres/Juhász
Yevtushenko

CHILDREN OF ALBION

Poetry of the 'Underground' in Britain

Edited by Michael Horovitz

Here at last is the 'secret' generation of British poets whose
work could hitherto be discovered only through their own bush
telegraph of little magazines and lively readings. These are the
energies which have almost completely dispelled the arid critical
climate of the 'fifties' and engineered a fresh renaissance of
'the voice of the bard' –

The anthology contains many of the best poems of

Pete Brown	Dave Cunliffe
Roy Fisher	Lee Harwood
Spike Hawkins	Anselm Hollo
Bernard Kops	Tom McGrath
Adrian Mitchell	Edwin Morgan
Neil Oram	Tom Pickard
Tom Raworth	Chris Torrance
Alex Trocchi	Gael Turnbull

– and *fifty* others – from John Arden to Michael X –

It is edited by Michael Horovitz, with a Blakean cornucopia
of 'afterwords' which trace the development of oral and jazz
poetry – the Albert Hall Incarnation of 1965 – the influences
of the great American and Russian spokesmen – and the diverse
lyric, political, visionary and revolutionary orientations of these
new poets.

POET TO POET

In the introductions to their personal selections from the work
of poets they have admired, the individual editors write as
follows:

Whitman selected by Robert Creeley

'If Whitman has taught me anything, and he has taught me a
great deal, often against my own will, it is that the common
is personal, intensely so, in that having no-one thus to invest it,
the sea becomes a curious mixture of water and table salt and
the sky the chemical formula for air. It is, paradoxically, the
personal which makes the common in so far as it recognizes the
existence of the many in the one. In my own joy or despair, I am
brought to that which others have also experienced.'

Wordsworth selected by Lawrence Durrell

'Wordsworth almost more than any other English poet enjoyed
a sense of inner confirmation – the mysterious sense of election
to poetry as a whole way of life. He realized too that one cannot
condescend to nature – one must work for it like a monk over
a missal which he will not live to see finished.'

POET TO POET

In the introductions to their personal selections from the work of poets they have admired, the individual editors write as follows:

Crabbe selected by C. Day Lewis

'As his poetry displays a balance and decorum in its versification, so his moral ideal is a kind of normality to which every civilized being should aspire. This, when one looks at the desperate expedients and experiments of poets (and others) today, is at least refreshing.'

Henryson selected by Hugh MacDiarmid

'There is now a consensus of judgement that regards Henryson as the greatest of our great makars. Literary historians and other commentators in the bad period of the century preceding the twenties of our own century were wont to group together as the great five: Henryson, Dunbar, Douglas, Lyndsay, and King James I; but in the critical atmosphere prevailing today it is clear that Henryson (who was, with the exception of King James, the youngest of them) is the greatest.'

Tennyson selected by Kingsley Amis

'England notoriously had its doubts as well as its certainties, its neuroses as well as its moral health, its fits of gloom and frustration and panic as well as its complacency. Tennyson is the voice of those doubts and their accompaniments, and his genius enabled him to communicate them in such a way that we can understand them and feel them as our own. In short we know from experience just what he means. Eliot called him the saddest of all English poets, and I cannot improve on that judgement.'